A Call to Action

A Call to Action

Frank V. Manning

Fides/Claretian
Notre Dame, Indiana 46556

© Copyright 1977: Fides/Claretian
Notre Dame, Indiana 46556

Photos by Ed Lettau

323
M 31

Library of Congress Cataloging in Publication Data
Manning, Frank V
    A call to action.

    1. Catholic Church in the United States—Congresses.
2. Church and social problems—Catholic Church—Con-
gresses. I. Title.
BX1404.M36   261'.0973   77-13092
ISBN 0-8190-0622-X

10775

Contents

Foreword

Catholics who read newspaper accounts of A CALL TO ACTION, the National Conference of Catholic Bishops' conference on liberty and justice held in Detroit last October, and who believed or were bewildered by those accounts, will find Frank Manning's brief work, *A CALL TO ACTION: An Interpretive Summary,* a stimulating surprise. Although nearly a year has elapsed since the CALL TO ACTION delegates assembled in Detroit's Cobo Hall to make their recommendations to the nation's bishops, Manning's book represents the first serious attempt to interpret and integrate those recommendations in a format usable on the parish or diocesan level.

Judging from the press following the CALL TO ACTION Conference one might have concluded that the majority of the topics debated there related to sex or to women: birth control, optional celibacy, homosexuality, the ERA, the ordination of women, divorce. Manning puts those important issues in perspective and goes on to draw out the material on family life, the problems of the young and of the aging, the political responsibility of the church, the plight of decaying neighborhoods, the issues of war and peace, and the concern for the negative impact of media and of consumerism. His summaries make clear the spirit of the justice conference, as well as the content:

—that the *church* be itself just, as well as an instrument of justice.

—that the *neighborhood* church be servant, *of* the neighborhood as well as *in* the neighborhood.

—that the freedom of the sons and daughters of God demands a chance for the full actualization of the human *person.*

—that *families* are communities who minister to others and who must be sustained by church.

—that the policy of the *nation* must reverence human life at every age and in every place.

—that *ethnic and racial* discrimination is social sin.

—that the *world* waits for the church and Christians, disciples of the Prince of Peace, to call for peace.

—that our present *economic* system keeps many poor and makes few rich.

The author takes the eight topic areas discussed in Detroit (Family, Personhood, Church, Neighborhood, Nationhood, Ethnicity and Race, Work and Humankind) and casts each in the framework of one of the eight beatitudes. In most cases, the parallels are clear and striking. The Family material, framed in the context of "Blessed are the merciful for they shall receive mercy," or the Nationhood resolutions grouped under, "Blessed are the peacemakers for they shall be called children of God," assume new significance as the author reflects the light of the gospel plan of Jesus for liberty and justice for all on recommendations coming from the CALL TO ACTION Conference.

In addition to drawing parallels between the CALL
TO ACTION material and the beatitudes, Manning
offers a clear summary of the resolutions included in
each of the eight topic areas, probably the best offered
by any author so far. He also provides a series of questions for discussion and issues for action for each of the
eight themes. It is clear that the book is intended for a
grass roots audience. The illustrations used by the author, the discussion questions, and the suggestions for
action are all geared to parish or diocesan response.
Perhaps the greatest service Manning has provided is
breaking the several hundred CALL TO ACTION resolutions down to language, format, and content that
Catholics on the local level will find practical. If the
Catholic community is to take seriously Cardinal Dearden's words at the close of the CALL TO ACTION
Conference:

> . . . As official delegates you must go back to your dioceses,
> your organizations and your friends to tell them what has
> happened here. We must tell those to whom we are ac-
> countable what we pledge ourselves to do. We must strug-
> gle and continue this process of speaking and listening and
> find even more effective mechanisms for deliberation, de-
> cision, collaborative action . . .

then Frank Manning has provided those delegates, and
the church at large, with a tool to make the task possible.

MARGARET CAFFERTY, PBVM
EXECUTIVE DIRECTOR
CATHOLIC COMMITTEE ON URBAN MINISTRY

Introduction

Contemporary research has been able to isolate two fundamental tensions present in all human relationships, that of dominance-submission, and that of love-hate. That is, in every interpersonal relationship, issues of control of the relationship and of the degree of mutual affection and respect between the parties have to be resolved. Power will either be shared equally, or one individual will dominate the other—at least with regard to specific areas of competence or control. The parties implicated in the relationship will either be united in intimacy, or will be distant from one another—in some measure lying along the love-hate spectrum.

These tensions arise from the very structure of the human person. Because all humans share the same nature, we are able to fuse in love. Because each of us is to some degree unique, our differences can serve either to separate or unite us, and the possibilities of hatred and dominance become significant. We are capable either of valuing our differences in such a way as to augment mutual respect and the cohesion of love, or we may view differences as threatening, react to them with hostility, and endeavor to control them by enforcing uniformity.

1

Thus we are confronted with the challenges of *liberty* and *justice*. Ultimately, liberty has to do with the possibility of fulfilling our potential as unique individuals. Justice, on the other hand, acts to counterbalance liberty. Justice demands that no individual's liberty be exalted at the expense of the basic rights of others. The function of justice is to assure that all human resources are so distributed and administered as to provide the minimal conditions necessary for all of us to strive to achieve our potential *together.* At this point justice merges into love, as we are enabled to reach higher levels of human liberty by "self-sacrifice," so that others less fortunate than ourselves may receive the minimum they need in order to live in a manner in keeping with their dignity as human persons. This is not the distorted sacrifice of self which diminishes the individual, but is that evangelical love by which we find ourselves in surrendering ourselves—for the sake of the gospel.

Since the church is comprised of human persons, and is in this sense subject to the inevitable limitations of the human factors affecting all organizations, it has not perfectly resolved within itself the tensions of dominance-submission and love-hate. It has not always been able adequately to reconcile the sometimes conflicting demands of "unity" and "pluralism." It has not, even in terms of its own structures and behaviors, been able to secure liberty and justice for its faithful. It has, to this degree, been restricted in its ability to strive for liberty and justice on behalf of humankind.

The church, as was made so evident by Vatican II, is ever in need of reform; it is the people of God *in progress;* a society of sinners—struggling to become a community of saints. While it has been able to enunciate the imperatives of justice and liberty in impressive theoretical utterances, the greatest obstacle, of course, remains the translation of such idealism into concrete policies, with all the practical ramifications that follow in the way of allocation of resources, and so on.

In a courageous effort to come to grips with this challenge, the bishops of the United States initiated a process unprecedented in the history of the Catholic church in this nation, a bicentennial consultation designated *A Call to Action*. Cardinal John Dearden, at the inauguration of the consultation in February, 1975, aptly capsulated the rationale and goal of the venture:

> In the bicentennial effort which we are beginning today, the bishops of the United States invite others to join in the widest possible sharing of assessments of how the American Catholic community can contribute to the quest of all people for liberty and justice. Today, as citizens of a democratic society and members of an interdependent human community, we must assume our full share of responsibility for the economic, political and cultural betterment of all persons (WP-I, 1).*

Cardinal Dearden's proposition is heavy with meaning and implication. Beyond the stated goals of liberty and justice, vital choices underlie the terms "interde-

*Throughout our study citations of the consultation's *Working Papers* will be abbreviated WP, followed by I, *Introduction*, C, *Church*, F, *Family*, NE, *Neighborhood*, W, *Work*, E, *Ethnicity and Race*, P, *Personhood*, NA, *Nationhood*, and H, *Humankind*, depending on which paper is being referenced. References to the *Call to Action* documents will be abbreviated CA, and will be taken from the *Origins* reprints, Vol. 6, Nos. 20, 21 of the *N C Documentary Service*.

pendent," "democratic," "economic," "American Catholic," "responsibility," and "for all." It is recognized that the Catholic church, a religious community, has secular concerns and responsibilities, because its members are at the same time citizens of a democratic society and interdependent world. It is declared that the church has, as part of its mission, a contribution to make toward the solution of economic, political, and cultural problems, and that decision making in this regard will include a process of serious dialogue and sharing on the widest attainable scale. The ultimate objective of the process and its aftermath, however, do not envision simply the sanctification of the faithful, or even the improvement of social conditions in the United States, but "the betterment of all persons." At the root of this universalism one witnesses both awareness of the de facto interdependence of all world citizens in the one family of humankind, and longing for fusion of all in the people of God, a fusion that unites and enriches legitimate differences.

Since its inauguration, *A Call to Action* has indeed been an active process, realized through incessant dialogue, listening, and feedback. Discussions have taken place at parish levels; one international and six national hearings have been conducted in the presence of representatives of the U.S. Conference of Catholic Bishops, and a wide variety of both "grassroots" people and specialists have submitted their testimony. Finally, the results of these preparatory efforts were brought together in the first national assembly of the American Catholic community at the *Call to Action* conference in Detroit, Michigan, Oct. 21-23, 1976.

From the some 1300 delegates participating in the conference there emerged 29 recommendations, subdivided into 218 specific action resolutions. The aim of obtaining "the widest possible sharing of assessments of how the American Catholic community can contribute to the quest of all people for liberty and justice" was largely met. Input was received from approximately 125 dioceses and 100 national organizations. In addition to the contributions of the delegates 1200 observers were present and had their influence on the proceedings.

While no pretense was made that the recommendations, or even the process as a whole, were scientifically representative of the opinions of the Catholic population as a whole, the assessment of the demands of justice and liberty was made, and stands as a mandate to the church's leadership. "Tell us your needs," the latter asked. The people spoke, and their needs were articulated.

From its inception it was understood that the bicentennial process was *consultative.* The power to act on the resolutions remains almost exclusively with the bishops. Yet the hope endures that, in the words of the *Introduction* to the *Working Papers,*

> These recommendations will form the basis for a five year pastoral plan by which the American church will then attempt to move directly and effectively to help bring about a greater degree of liberty and justice for all (WP-I, 2).

The fundamental purpose of this essay will be to reflect on the content of the action resolutions produced by the consultation. Media reports on the Detroit assembly tended to single out for comment a few of the more "exotic" resolutions. Rarely was justice done to the comprehensiveness and overall balance of the recommendations for action approved by the delegation. The aspiration here will be to bring into focus the central concerns voiced in the resolutions, making manifest both the general moderateness of the delegates, and also the sense of urgency with which they called for unequivocal, timely *action*.

Moderation, to be sure, is not to be identified with complacency with the status quo. If one emphasis unmistakably crystallized from the two years of deliberation, it was *impatience*. The church may not, and in fact does not, have "solutions" in hand for the many complex problems confronted by *A Call to Action*. Participants in the process, however, demonstrated clearly that much of the church's leadership, lay as well as religious or clerical, does have a definite idea of where we need to *begin*. The consensus is ominous in its persuasion that undue delay or temporizing will be disastrous.

It will not be possible to treat the resolutions of the conference exhaustively. Rather, the "essential impact" of the series of actions proposed will be distilled and summarized, with a view toward recommending several priorities for action which might influence the five year plan mentioned above. An attempt will be made to indicate the way in which the resolutions respond to the tensions between dominance-submission, love-hate, unity and diversity, and justice and liberty alluded to earlier.

The schema of the commentary will follow that of the *Working Papers* and the conference itself, in the sense that both treat eight topics: Church, Family, Neighbor-

hood, Work, Ethnicity and Race, Personhood, Nationhood, and Humankind. This sequence, however, will be
reviewed within the biblical framework offered by the
eight beatitudes. The parallel may at times seem somewhat forced, but the underlying commonality of values
is unquestionable. The sermon on the mount, and the
beatitudes in particular, constitute the "manifesto" of
Jesus Christ for liberty and justice in the world, the
reign of God on behalf of the powerless and dispos-
sessed. *A Call to Action,* in its eight sections, is a *mandate* setting forth what the beatitudes imply for Christian
commitment, as the Catholic church moves toward its
twenty-first century.

1

Church

"Blessed are they who hunger and thirst after justice, for they shall be filled" (Mt. 5:6).*

Traditionally it has been theologically acceptable to distinguish between justice and love. "Justice" was then taken to delimit a minimal type of behavior "sufficient" to skirt the boundaries of sinfulness. Actually, as the Christian conscience matures, it takes the beatitudes more seriously and finds it more difficult to draw an easy distinction between justice and love. Thus we find in the *Working Papers* on *Church* the statement, "Justice should not be understood simply as a system of legal safeguards against oppression, but also a set of loving relationships by which people are united under God" (WP-C, 16). It is this spirit that runs through the various resolutions emerging from this section of *Call to Action*.

*Even though contemporary versions of the New Testament are generally to be preferred, I have chosen to retain the traditional wording. It is currently in fashion to replace the term "blessed" with "happy." Unfortunately, the notion of "happiness" is too contaminated by materialistic connotations to be susceptible to communicating the sense of "blessedness" intended by earlier translators. "Happiness" for us suggests physical contentment or, at best, psychological well-being. To be "blessed," on the other hand, may include being miserable on an earthly scale of values and yet experiencing the fullness of life that is given by grace alone.

9

It was keenly perceived throughout the consultation process and in the conference itself that if the church is to be an effective instrument for the achievement of liberty and justice, its own inner life must be a credible reflection of the gospel it proclaims. The stress of *Church*, then, is not on the many positive aspects of contemporary Catholic ecclesial activity, but on those areas where we urgently need to "mend our fences," or perhaps dismantle them altogether.

Suggestions for social justice initiatives with regard to the church itself, submitted by parishioners across the nation, outnumbered all others. The recommendations which integrate their input, and that of other dimensions of the consultation, fall into three areas: justice in the church, women in the church, and education.

Justice in the Church

The insistence upon coresponsibility and sharing in decision making in the church, present throughout *Call to Action*, finds its most vigorous expression here. Concern is voiced that the church act justly by acknowledging and using the *full* supply of gifts and talents available. "Ministry is exercised through various apostolates and services not only by the ordained clergy but also by lay persons as well. These ministries should be recognized and honored in all our action resolutions in the interest of justice in the church" (CA-C, 309).

The demands of justice are to be pursued studiously with respect to the church's use of its financial resources. Such resources should be allocated more sensitively, in light of *gospel* values, especially in response to the needs of the poor. In this instance, as in many others, conference delegates called for structures, e.g., parish and diocesan pastoral councils, to assure implementation. In another dimension, that of the just treatment of *human* resources, establishment of a national review board for due process was urged.

Impatience with a so-called "geographic morality" governing annulment of marriages was made quite clear. The inequity of harsh vs. liberal policies in different dioceses is understandably deeply troubling to many. Implementation of "current jurisprudence in all diocesan marriage tribunals throughout the nation" is advocated (CA-C, 311).

Another area of injustice in the church has to do with various brands of discrimination. Every vestige of institutional prejudice and discrimination must be eliminated, and displaced by positive actions. Thus there should be adequate training and preparation of ministers for multidimensional pastoral care, responsive to the needs of diverse racial, ethnic, and cultural groups.

A fundamental responsibility of the church is to proclaim and teach the Word with integrity. Delegates intimated widespread misgivings about shortcomings here, on two levels: the lack of clarity of theological teaching on the part of church leaders, and the poor quality of homilies. The difficulty of integrating clarity with pluralism, or legitimate differences of opinion, is acknowledged. It seems that the boundaries within which theological discussion is free to range are currently hazy; in reality, not only the scope but the very nature of the boundaries may be changing. Delegates, and the consultation as a whole, do not appear to be anxious to define such limits narrowly, but appealed for a more effective articulation of what constitutes responsible freedom of speech within the church.

An intense desire was also advanced for justice as it bears upon the question of who will have access to the ministry. The possibility of a twofold injustice may be inferred: pressing needs are not being met because of a shortage of ministers; simultaneously, capable individuals, fully willing to serve, are being denied access to the ministry—possibly because of no longer tenable reasons. The delegates, therefore, asserted themselves strongly in favor of ordination of women and of married men, while also recommending that priests be allowed to exercise the right to marry and remain in or resume the active priesthood.

While it was evident that *Call to Action* participants were surprisingly united in their support of the above changes, at the same time they sought orderly development through recognized institutional channels, requesting for example that "the NCCB initiate dialogue with Rome to change the present discipline in the Western Rite of the Roman Catholic Church to allow women to be ordained to the diaconate and priesthood" (CA-C, 317). The latter recommendation is a rather characteristic illustration of the way in which the delegates sharpened and rendered more "actionable" the language of the original draft, which read: "Immediate attention should be given to the impact on this right to competent pastoral care of the present restrictions relative to married clergy and the ordination of women to the priesthood and diaconate" (WP-C, 19).

Women in the Church

Pervasive in the document *Church* is the theme of building community, vitally alive Christian community. Attention, as a matter of course, focuses upon traits of the contemporary church which are conducive to devisiveness and undermine community. Along with racial and ethnic prejudices, and the general withholding from the faithful of a justly proportionate role of participation in policy making and administration, traditional church life and practice are criticized for having "limited the freedom of women to share responsibility and ministry" (CA-C, 312). It seems probable that this is currently *the* most serious obstacle to getting on with the task of revitalization of community and Christian life within the U.S. Catholic church.

The delegation here too appeals for structural reforms and/or innovations. The bishops are asked "to establish within the NCCB/USCC an effectively staffed structure to promote the full participation of women in the life and ministry of the church." (CA-C, 312). The NCCB and local bishops are urged to develop, together with representative women, an affirmative action plan to assure the equal status of women in the church, including full access to ecclesial training and leadership functions.

One resolution approved at this point reveals both the agreement in general orientation of the delegates and a certain lack of logical consistency. Earlier it was suggested (by a different working committee) that dialogue should be instituted with Rome, to move towards the ordination of women. Yet here it is resolved that a careful interpretive study be carried out, to facilitate "a more fully developed position on the ordination of women to sacred orders" (CA-C, 312). Obviously, many if not most of the delegates had already concluded that women should have access to sacred orders; the purpose of the recommended study could only be to confirm the rightness and justice of this desire.

It is noteworthy that even at the *Working Papers* level the recommendation with regard to women in the church was already incisively formulated. The amending process had the effect of making the sense of urgency more palpable, and of further specifying details with regard to institutionalizing the process of change. All in all, this was probably the least amended recommendation of the conference. A high degree of consensus and lack of ambivalence is thereby demonstrated. The delegates, if not always perfectly logical, were clear on what is desired: full, equal participation of women in the entire life of the people of God, in accordance with sound scriptural and theological tradition.

Education

Several sectors are pinpointed in which insufficient attention to justice has frustrated the impact of the church's teaching endeavors. The most numerous suggestions offered during the consultation process centered upon adult education. The implication is that the needs of adults have been neglected. Either they have not been considered at all, or, when they have been addressed, the approach has been paternalistic. It is resolved, therefore, that "very high priority be given adult formation, appropriate to the needs and concerns of the total church and the people involved, respecting the principles of adult learning." Adult lay Catholics, furthermore, should be involved in participative decision making in the determination of "total Catholic educational policies at the local and diocesan level" (CA-C, 313).

Other justice issues mentioned indicate the need not only to purge all forms of educational discrimination, but equally to provide constructive programs relevant to "racial, ethnic, and cultural concerns." Special efforts of support should be developed where the local community is too poor to finance Catholic schools.

Two contrasting anxieties surface: a) That educational programs are not adequately attuned to the local parish's needs. Not corresponding to a locally felt need, they fail to evoke interest or support. b) That the parish might become overly self-centered. Consciousness of the interdependence of its own health and the social well-being of the world beyond parish boundaries must direct educational efforts of the parish community.

Similarly, bifocal concern for both Catholic *and* public education is evidenced. Delegates call for a nondenominational national organization to seek public funding in support of the exercise of the right of religious freedom with regard to choice of schools. That is, tax revenue should be available for the establishment and maintenance of nonpublic schools. At the same time, the church should give proof of its interest in public education. Catholics, as citizens, should take a more active role in exercising leadership and formulating policy with regard to issues of justice, for example, racial integration, moral aspects of education in the public schools, and so on.

A final preoccupation, uttered several times and stressed here, highlights discontent with the way homilies are handled. The criticism seems to be at two levels: It targets on the *way* (content and method) homilies are delivered, and on the "by whom" (clerics only). The inference may be drawn that the responsibility for proclaiming the Word could be better met by improved training and ongoing evaluation, and by allowing competent nonclerics to deliver homilies when the circumstances are appropriate.

The recommendations approved under the section *Church,* then, basically orient our attention to the church's inner life. A firm foundation of justice within must precede and undergird the mission of the people of God to bring justice to the world. Unless we hunger and thirst after justice for ourselves and those closest to us, how can we presume to struggle for justice on behalf of others? Or if we do—who will believe us?

Questions for Discussion:

1. In your parish and diocese, has the church acted justly in the use made of the talents and gifts of its members?
2. What does it mean to allocate resources in light of gospel values? What values do you think are relevant?
3. What is the need for "due process" in the church?
4. How do you feel about the church's treatment of

those in troubled marriages, or divorced and remarried Catholics?

5. Do you believe women should have access to sacred orders, and participate fully in all roles and functions of the church's life?

6. What do you feel is the proper role of the parish with regard to secular education?

Issues for Action:

1. What can you do in your parish to encourage a more just use of personal talent and ability? In improving homilies? In other educational efforts? In parish management?

2. How can your parish improve the ways in which it shares its resources with the poor? What can the diocese do?

3. What steps can your parish take toward the formation of an active and effective Diocesan Pastoral Council?

4. What can you and your parish do toward the enrichment of marriage and increased pastoral care for those with marital problems?

5. What can be done within your parish to assure equal treatment for women, both in religious and secular matters?

6. Would your parish share in a diocesan/national effort to obtain tax revenue for private schools?

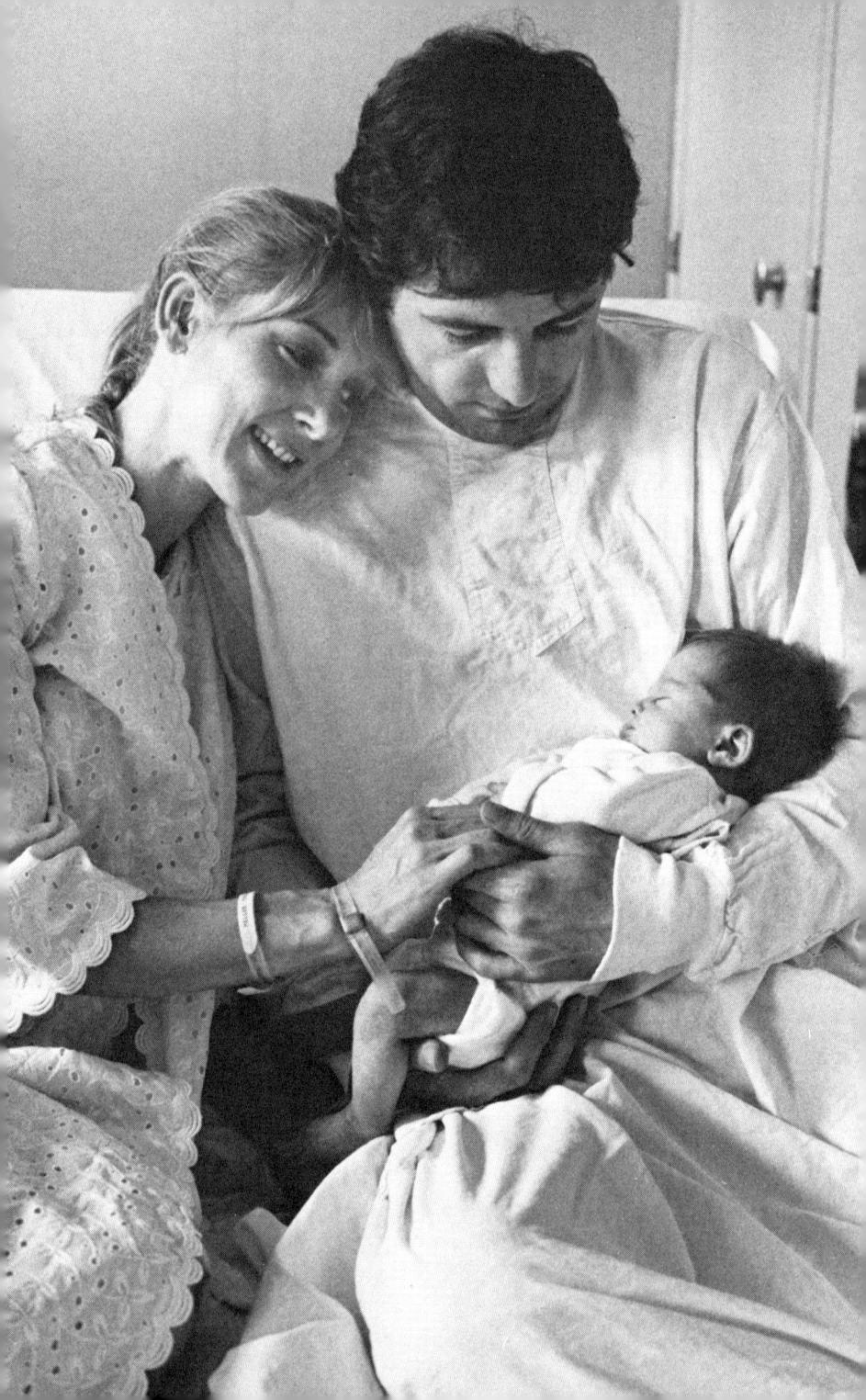

2

Family

"Blessed are the merciful, for they shall obtain mercy" (Mt.5:7).

"Mercy" is frequently conceptualized as a sort of pity, the compassion of the victor for the vanquished, the condescension of the "righteous" for the "wicked." Actually it would seem much more scripturally valid and in keeping with the example of Christ to conceive of "mercy," as unconditional love, receiving all and reaching out to all. It is this kind of mercy that permeates *Call to Action's* view of marriage and the family.

The *Working Paper* on *Family* notes that "the American Catholic church has a rich heritage of support for family life" (WP-F, 1). The structures of parishes and parochial schools have served to strengthen family life. It is observed that Catholic parishes have been "networks of families... connected to one another through the parish, reaching out to encompass the elderly, the orphan, and sometimes, but not always, the unmarried" (WP-F, 2).

Historically, however, the quality of mercy has not always accompanied the church's treatment of families in difficulty, as " . . . families who survived, and the pastors who served them, saw the failure of others as rooted simply in weakness of character, in sin." "So the moral, religious, and social support system the church provided for families was often limited by parochialism, ethnic self-righteousness, and a peculiarly American emphasis on character, rather than condition, as the key to family success and failure" (WP-F, 2).

In our times the institutions of marriage and the family stand at a new crossroads. Their existence has been threatened before and their disappearance forecast. Currently, however, the dimensions of the crisis may be considered unprecedented. In response to the situation, we find in the consultation process not a gloomy pessimism nor elite self-righteousness, but a reaffirmation of "the importance and value of family life, while exploring new models of family life which embrace the dignity and work of each member." At the same time, a new awareness of the special needs of the childless, the widowed, the divorced, and the single is in evidence (WP-F, 2).

Throughout *Call to Action* the mission of the church to create and sustain community is a continual theme. This is particularly true with regard to the community of the family. The one suggestion which outnumbered all others in the consultation was directed toward support of marriage and family life—in an appeal to the church to provide opportunities for family activities and sharing. The resolutions decipher in some detail the content of such opportunities. They are organized under three headings: support for family values, family and society, and the church and divorced Catholics.

Support for Family Values

The prologue to this recommendation reaffirms the permanence, indissolubility, and sacramentality of marriage, manifesting that all which follows is to be interpreted in light of these basic values of the Christian faith. This recommendation and the two that accompany it, moreover, accurately reflect the observation in the *Working Paper* that "family life is a convergent issue for Catholics, pulling them together in a shared concern across barriers that sometimes divide them," so that, notwithstanding the need to defend the institutions of marriage and family in contemporary society, the people of the church "don't want a negative approach which emphasizes how badly off the family is in today's world and that attacks the supposed sins of divorce and sexual selfishness. They do respond to the positive approach of Vatican II which emphasizes human growth, conjugal love and fidelity, personal and family responsibility, and mutual support within the community of faith" (WP-F, 8).

The resolutions vary from identification of specific values to be fostered to structures and policies needed for implementation. Among the values found in Christian marriage should be the "expression of the creative fruitfulness of human life and love" (CA-F, 317), the finding of fulfillment in service to others, the actualization of personal potential, the affirmation of cultural heritage and diversity. There is, on the other hand, the concomitant need to join with others in combatting social, economic, and cultural forces threatening family life. Catholics, as well as other religious and civic groups, must become involved in the formulation of public policy and social legislation which contribute to the strengthening of marriage and family life. Within the church, further development of the theology of marriage and refinement of catechesis at all levels is regarded as essential.

To implement pursuit of the above goals and values, delegates call for relevant structures and planning. A comprehensive pastoral plan for family ministry must be generated. It will include a standing committee of the NCCB with responsibility for marriage and family life. The plan will be formulated in collaboration with competent laity and family members. Efforts will extend to the establishment and support of diocesan family life offices, with family life liaison officers.

Decisions and activities emanating from such an effort would include just allocation of church resources for family ministry programs, recognition of the competency of permanent deacons and lay people, further development of family-centered worship and religious education, formation of family support groups for prayer, preparation for marriage, marriage enrichment, and so on.

Family and Society

Recommendation II recognizes that the Christian family can remain sound and become Christian, in fact as well as in name, only by becoming involved in a commitment that stretches beyond its own immediate interests. Church programs, then, should contribute to rendering families aware of the needs of others, whether on a local or international level. Christian ministry should be directed toward strong marriages, as well as toward those in difficulty, to enable all families "to open them-

selves to the injustices in the world," not simply to become more aware, but to be enabled to engage in
problem-solving *action* (CA-F, 319).

Families, as part of the entire Catholic community,
should concern themselves with public policy and social
legislation fostering human rights and social justice. On
the structural level, the NCCB and dioceses must "work
out mechanisms for organizing families into coalitions
on family-related issues." The establishment of pastoral
councils on nation to neighborhood levels is urged to
this end (CA-F, 319).

A specific concern here is the impact of mass media
on family life, especially apropos the "dehumanizing
values of consumerism and materialism" and the por-
trayal of "excessive violence and irresponsible sex"
(CA-F, 319). Through coalitions and similar organizations families should not only combat these harmful influ-
ences, but should also unite in support of programming
which reinforces family values.

The Church and Divorced Catholics

The section on *Family* closes with a firm pledge to
strive for reconciliation of separated, divorced, and
divorced/remarried Catholics. The consultation process
as a whole and the conference in particular agree in
acknowledging that Catholics in every area of the
church have participated in injustices towards those individuals whose marriages have ended in separation of
one form or another. Reconciliation, therefore, does not
signify condescension toward the sinner; rather, it envi-

sions reunion and mutual support of the imperfect with the imperfect, of the sinful with the sinful, *all* to be forgiven by the same Lord.

Effective programs of pastoral care for the separated, divorced, and divorced/remarried are to be designed and implemented. Practices which stigmatize and discriminate are to be ended. Church leaders are exhorted to "address the request of the divorced who have remarried to receive, under certain conditions, the sacraments of the church" (CA-F, 319). Delegates appeal to the bishops for more equitable, pastorally oriented procedures governing annulment and dissolution of marriages. It is suggested that serious study of the causes of marital breakdown, using the resources of the victims of broken marriages, will lead to more realistic policies for reinforcing family life. Finally, the bishops are asked to repeal the penalty of automatic excommunication for Catholics who remarry after divorce.*

It is important to note that, in contrast with other sections of *Call to Action,* that of *Family* did not add or delete any resolutions as such in the conference's revision process. A singular degree of consensus was present relative to family issues. In general the changes introduced were in the sense of being more inclusive of those to be served and more emphatic about the right

---

*It should be observed that in their initial response to *A Call to Action* the bishops have acted favorably on this suggestion. Other recommendations, however, have generally been referred to specialized committees for further consideration.

and responsibility of the laity to share and exercise their expertise in the domain of marriage and family life. Without exception, the tone of mercy as the outreach of unconditional love prevailed.

Questions for Discussion:

1. Why do you think Catholics look toward the parish to provide means of strengthening family life?
2. What impact do you think public policy and social legislation have on family life? What specific policies and laws do you think are important in this regard?
3. Do you feel that worship can really have a useful role to play in building family unity?
4. Can you think of any ways in which the soundness of family life is influenced by the needs of others— outside of the parish, or even the nation?
5. How has mass media affected the quality of your family life?
6. Do you feel that Catholics who have divorced and remarried should be allowed to receive the eucharist? Why or why not? Under any conditions?

Issues for Action:

1. What can your parish/diocese do to provide activities encouraging family unity and sharing?
2. What can you or your parish do to change a particular law or policy which is harmful to family life? To foster legislation that would be more positive?
3. Create a worship service that highlights and uses family involvement in an innovative way, or to a new degree.

4. Design a parish program to help a group in need outside of the parish—utilizing family efforts to plan and carry out the design.
5. Form a coalition of families to take some kind of action to affect the media, even if it is simply a social contract to watch certain types of programming and to boycott others.
6. What has your parish done, or what will it do to improve its ministry to the single, separated, and divorced/remarried?

3

Neighborhood

"Blessed are those who are persecuted for the
sake of justice, for theirs is the kingdom of
heaven (Mt. 5:10).

Historically the Catholic church, through its parish
structure, has been neighborhood centered. As the
Working Paper on *Neighborhood* expresses it: "In many
ways beyond worship and devotional activities, the
parish was the center of the neighborhood.... The
instrument for sharing was often the parish, with all
its facilities from altar to gymnasium" (WP-NE, 1).
Technological advances and the consequent urbaniza-
tion, however, have vastly altered life styles and community patterns, disrupting earlier cohesive networks in
an endless multitude of ways. Still, "new forms of community life seem less attractive; no substitute for the
neighborhood has appeared to fulfill the age-old quest
for community" (WP-NE, 2). Notwithstanding the
avalanche of material advantages brought by modern
living, other values have been sacrificed, human values
of intimacy, mutual caring, and support. The result has
been intense suffering, in a sense "persecution" of ourselves, the victims of our own success and affluence.
Those who have carried the heaviest burden of the injustices making possible much of our astounding rate of
material progress, of course, have been the poor and

powerless. For the sake of justice, the time for those who have been more fortunate to share in their persecution has come—by risking the changes which must be made. In the word of Pope Paul VI:

> There is an urgent need to remake at the level of the street, of the neighborhood ... the social fabric whereby individuals may be able to develop the needs of their personalities. . . . To build up the city, the place where men and women and their expanded communities exist, to create new modes of neighborliness and relationships, to perceive an original application of social justice and to undertake responsibility for this collective future, which is foreseen as difficult, is a task in which Christians must share. . . . This can be done by brotherhood which is lived and by concrete justice" (Quoted in WP-NE, 2).

The gospel bestows its blessing on those who are persecuted for the sake of justice. In large part, however, the drama of deteriorating neighborhoods has been a history of persecution because of injustices. The poor suffer that the affluent might prosper. The affluent suffer, tormented by their own anonymity and suburban alienation. The voices of the suffering, then, are not slow to echo the words of Paul VI. Again and again participants of the consultation on neighborhood "call upon their church to fight crime, offer better services, share its resources with people in need, and bring people together. . . . The problems are the same in all urban neighborhoods: crime, poverty, health, housing, education, and the general lack of governmental responsiveness to human needs. In small towns and rural areas there are some similar problems, such as transportation, the aging, poverty, but there are unique special concerns: the decline of the family farm and the growth of concentrated ownership of natural resources, especially the land" (WP-NE, 4).

The inference is that the church can only legitimize its teachings on Christian justice and love, can only *be* the servant church, by directing its influence and resources toward solving *local* problems. One witness spelled out four specific roles for the church in this respect: "One is an *advocate*. The church can see itself as a protector of rights of the poor. It can speak to and *identify moral issues* which are important today. It can be an *organizer* in the sense it can help to convene people and form coalitions which are necessary to meet head on those people who are restricting people from decent housing. It can be an *innovator*. It can develop new programs" (WP-NE, 5, emphasis added). Some thirty-eight concrete proposals were offered in response to these challenges.

The Parish and the Neighborhood

As the family and parish/neighborhood are potentially closely related communities, the concerns here are similar to those found under *Family*. Thus the recommendation seeks to render the parish a more volatile catalyst for revitalization of neighborhood community life. Liturgies should become celebrations of community life and neighborliness. Equally, the sacramental and prayer life of the neighborhood church are to reflect the relationship between Christian commitment and community realities. Parish social action should be typified by personalized outreach, for example, by including "ministry to the alienated, mentally, physically, and socially handicapped, and any others whom society shuns" (CA-NE, 320).

Through the amendment process of the conference it became clear that general awareness needs to be made more acute in this domain, hence, training of parish leadership is recommended. Talents of natural community leaders must be fully utilized. Thematic here is a less "clerical" neighborhood church, one that actively seeks out the opportunity to serve, as opposed to a parish waiting to be asked to intervene.

Church and Neighborhood Action

The neighborhood consciousness evoked above is, of course, only an initial step. Instruments need to be established to translate consciousness into action. The strategy is not for the church to develop "Catholic" action agencies, but to put its resources at the disposal of competent, broad-based neighborhood action groups. Emphasis is on cooperative effort *with* (not *for*) neighborhood forces as they exist and struggle, in all the complexity of their multicultural, pluralistic situations. Not only should facilities be shared, but budgetary items on the parish and diocesan balance sheets should assign financial support to competent neighborhood/community action groups. Each diocese, furthermore, is called upon to establish (or expand) an office for community affairs, to contribute institutional backup strength to comparable neighborhood offices.

The urgent needs within the inner city are especially noted. The delegates assert the situation "mandates that the church recognize inner city neighborhoods as territories demanding priority attention and . . . interim missionary personnel." The Catholic church should "pledge itself to remain as an active force in the inner city" (CA-NE, 321).

Finally, the needs of another neighborhood often neglected, the collegiate neighborhood, are recognized. A fixed portion of diocesan personnel and resources should be allocated for ministry on college and university campuses.

Church and Community Development

Justice requires not only that resources be distributed equitably, but also that in their allocation the dignity and competency of the supposed beneficiaries is not violated. Thus the *Call to Action* assembly voted that every diocese should undertake a self-study of the application of its resources, issue a full public report within one year, and develop within three years a plan of social justice, with an implementation schedule. In working out such policies and programs there should be included "a recognition and commitment in every diocese that community development must flow from the needs of the people *as identified by the people*" (CA-NE, 322, emphasis added). The church's aspiration should be to join in clearing the way for the empowerment of the powerless. Coresponsibility, therefore, is the keynote of all new endeavors.

The foundation for appropriate action can only be laid by education at all levels. Community participatory education is urged for neighborhood parishes, address-

ing both issues of local and larger social concern:
"... Immigration; delivery of services; quality of
education; the aged; youth and the handicapped; the
ownership and use of natural resources, including land,
as this relates especially to the worldwide crisis of food
and energy; race relations; crime; industrial and economic development" (CA-NE, 322). "Social justice
courses in the area of neighborhood parish community
development, community organization and multicultural
education," moreover, should "be mandatory in the
training of seminarians and in the continuing education
of clergy and religious" (CA-NE, 322).

To insure pursuit of the above goals, through public
and church related policies and programs, a variety of
institutional mechanisms is proposed, including a diocesan staff position to monitor public policy, and offices of
ministry to social concerns at the diocesan, state, and
national levels. At the same time, existing programs or
agencies (e.g., Catholic Charities, diocesan offices for
rural life, urban affairs, or social action, and the Campaign for Human Development) must receive more sub-
stantial support.

The Church and the Rural Community

It is plain from the tenor and content of the resolutions under this recommendation that rural areas
have in the past suffered from a kind of "benign neglect" on the part of the U.S. Catholic church, but that
the situation is changing—and must continue to change
still more rapidly. Delegates insist that church structures
and programs of ministry to rural communities be

evaluated and revamped so that improvement of the quality of life in rural areas becomes a priority concern and be acted upon through just distribution of resources.

The National Catholic Rural Life Conference should be strengthened and its efforts buttressed through diocesan Rural Life Offices. Such offices should seek legislation to halt the abuse of land speculation and exploitation of agricultural workers. From the bishops is requested a pastoral letter, witnessing to "the dignity of rural life for Christian living." Innovative structures/ ministries, "such as mobile teams of resource persons and new forms of lay leadership and ministry," should be attempted (CA-NE, 323).

The church must strive to assist in the amelioration of living and working conditions for all farm laborers, including but not limited to migrants, for example, by recognizing and encouraging their right to organize. The situations of the people of Appalachia and of undocumented aliens are singled out as particularly pressing. It is noted that a fair portion of Campaign for Human Development funds should be directed to community organizing activities in rural areas.

Ongoing Implementation

This recommendation was not included in the original *Working Paper,* but was added at the section level of the Detroit conference during the second revision. It is not as detailed, but essentially duplicates Recommendation IV under *Nationhood* (and will be discussed there). It would appear that the delegates intended this duplication for the purpose of underscoring the intensity of their desire for meaningful, timely action on these issues.

At the *Working Paper* stage *Neighborhood* already consisted of twenty-two action resolutions, a comparatively high number. Sixteen additional resolutions were introduced by way of amendment, testifying to the high level of concern and activity energizing this section. In sum, the resolutions depict in rather vivid detail the kinds of things which must be done if the Catholic church is to be one with those suffering persecution for the sake of justice, to be *of* the neighborhood and not merely *in* it, to identify with the poor and powerless—rather than remain simply an impassive establishment, awaiting and ministering only to the few who are so bold as to insist upon being helped.

Questions for Discussion:

1. What would you say is the most serious social problem in your neighborhood?
2. Does your parish have any "natural community leaders?" Is their leadership ability recognized and used by the church?
3. Are you familiar with any neighborhood action groups? Does your parish budget any funds for assistance to neighborhood social action?
4. What types of interaction exist between your parish/ diocese and the "inner city?" Do you think present efforts should be increased, remain the same, or decrease?

5. To what extent does coresponsibility exist in identifying and meeting neighborhood needs in your parish/diocese?
6. Do you believe you or your parish should take an interest in the quality of rural life in your diocese? Why or why not? Are you aware of the problems encountered by "undocumented immigrants?"

Issues for Action:

1. Design a parish activity to identify and increase awareness of at least one significant social problem in your neighborhood.
2. Survey your parish and neighborhood to ascertain knowledge and feelings about "natural community leaders" and their relationship to the church.
3. Evaluate your parish budget, and justify it in terms of whether it does enough to support neighborhood social action.
4. Carry out a carefully planned parish project to improve interaction between the inner city and other urban districts.
5. Devise a plan to increase the practice of coresponsibility in identifying and responding to neighborhood needs.
6. Generate a program to bring together representatives of rural and urban life, to increase mutual awareness and explore methods of problem solving with regard to specific issues.

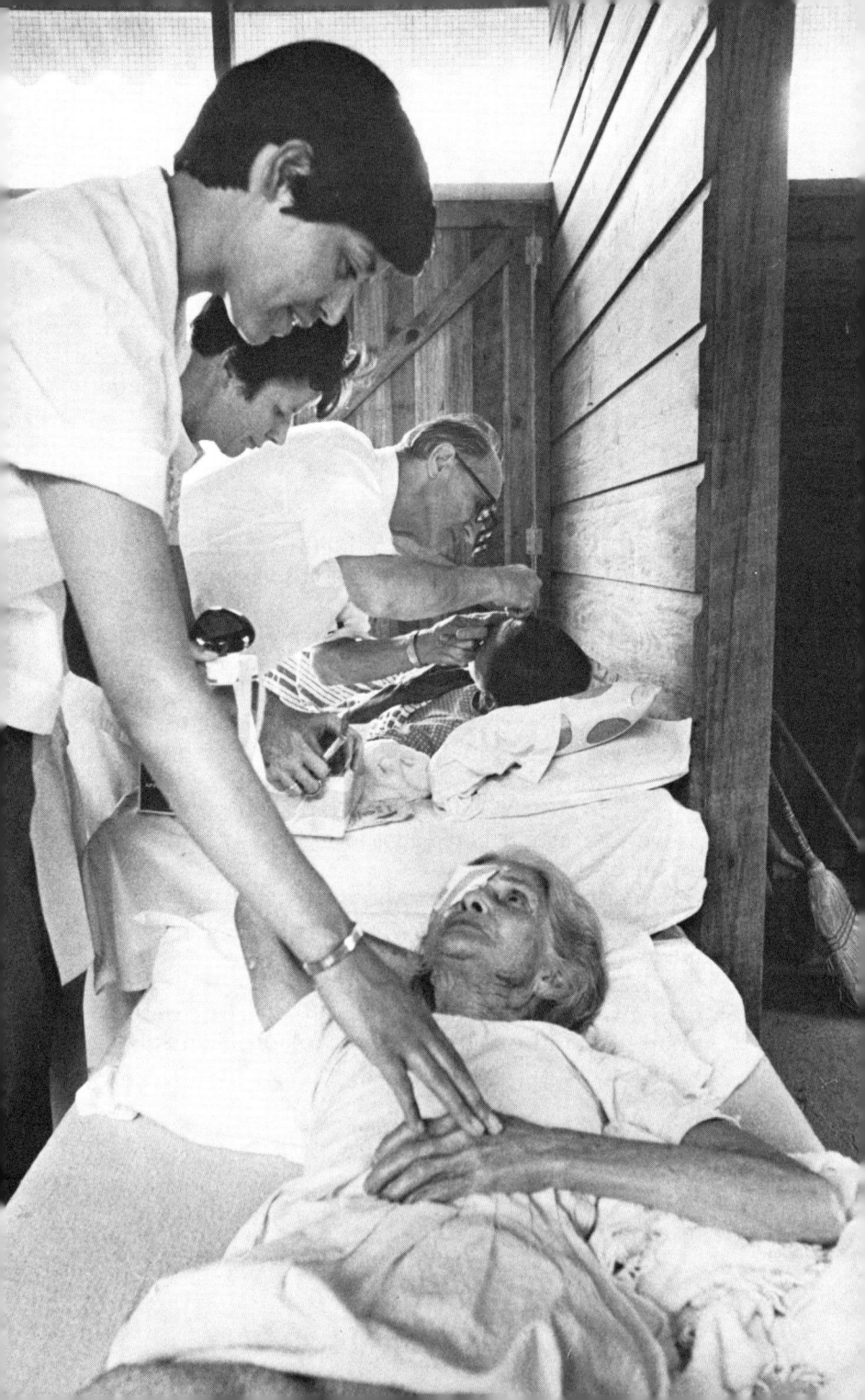

4

Work

"Blessed are the poor in spirit, for theirs is the
kingdom of heaven" (Mt. 5:3).

In the course of both the Old and New Testaments
God's special predilection for the poor, his *anawim*, is
continually reiterated. To be "poor in spirit," con-
sequently, is not to indulge in some kind of romantic
sympathy for the impoverished, it is to identify with the
powerless by entering into the world of their suffering
through costly sacrifice. Jesus Christ was "poor in spirit"
not because of an empty portfolio, but because he "emp-
tied himself of his Godhead," he united himself with
the disenfranchisement of the powerless—unto death.
Possibly this is not far from what the world synod of
bishops had in mind when it taught that "action for
justice is a constitutive dimension of the preaching of
the gospel" (quoted in WP-W, 13). Possibly this is what
was being urged upon the church itself, when the same
bishops

> said that 'while the church is bound to give witness to jus-
> tice, she recognizes that anyone who ventures to speak to
> people about justice must first be just in their eyes,' and that
> 'those who serve the church by their labor, including priests
> and religious, should receive a sufficient livelihood and
> enjoy that social security which is customary in their re-

gion,' that 'lay people should be given fair wages and a system for promotion,' and that 'lay people should exercise more important functions with regard to church property and should share in its administration' (WP-W, 11).

Call to Action participants who directed their concern to the dimension of work, did so with perceptive determination. Inequitable differences of income between minorities, women, and white male workers were pointed to. The high rate of unemployment, perhaps 50 percent higher in reality than government figures admit, was deplored. The lack of collective bargaining agreements to protect the working poor was signaled. Concentration of wealth, "with the top one-half of one percent of families owning more wealth than the bottom 81 percent was questioned (WP-W, 3).

In brief, the critical problem areas identified included: unemployment, inflation, inequality in the distribution and enjoyment of the nation's wealth, lack of meaning and purpose in many jobs, enforced early retirement, absence of worker representation through collective bargaining, and a tax system that "unduly burdens the poor and lower paid working persons in our country" (WP-W, 10).

Action resolutions in response to these challenges were included under four headings: equal opportunity; economic justice; responsibility in the world of work; apostolate and working life.

Equal Opportunity

The church is asked to engage, at all levels, in intense, systematic action to assure equal opportunity. An EEO program should be implemented immediately by the USCC, backed up by equal opportunity plans and affirmative action commissions in all dioceses. Activities of such instruments would include a continual survey of employees of Catholic institutions, to monitor equal opportunity in hiring and promotion practices. Accountability should be enforced through supervision of regular reports from each diocese, with reference to progress toward measurable and very detailed objectives for each parish.

Other specific actions for justice in this domain include the delegates' endorsement of and exhortation for tangible church support of the Equal Rights Amendment and the recommendation that Catholics exert economic influence to begin to reshape the orientation of large economic institutions, for example, using their power as shareholders to direct multinational corporations to function in such a way as to foster economic and social justice for all concerned, granted the necessity of making a reasonable return on investment.

Economic Justice

In essence this recommendation envisions the establishment, within one year of a commission on economic justice. The latter would follow up on the concerns identified in the statement of the U.S. bishops in 1975, *The Economy: Human Dimensions,* namely: "full employment, job training and development, income security, tax reform, the problem of over-employment, national standards for workmen's compensation and unemployment insurance" (CA-W, 4). International and domestic dimensions of economic problems are to be assessed, along with the study and evaluation of our economic system itself.

Other activities urged extend from committees on economic justice at the diocesan level, with grassroots representatives, to "economic justice forums to include stock-holders, management, labor, public interest and consumer groups, youth, and those involved in human services," to repeal of "Right to Work" laws as they now exist in twenty states (CA-W, 339).

Responsibility in the World of Work

Resolutions here are concrete and pointed. The Catholic community must recognize and support the right of its own employees to form and/or join unions. Church agencies should make resources available to assist in organizational efforts for all workers afflicted by an absence of adequate representation. Particular groups of workers are identified for support, for example, Vietnam era veterans, nonunion textile workers in the South, farmworkers throughout America, and undocumented immigrants. On behalf of the last group the church is asked to promote amnesty and to combat the abuse of human and civil rights deriving from "enforcement tactics" of the Immigration and Naturalization Service. Policies of multinational corporations which pressure "economic refugees" to emigrate to this country are to be exposed.

Not only should injustices be resisted, however, positive programs of collaboration with business need to be initiated. "... The church should encourage efforts at labor-management cooperation including research and prudent experimentation on profit sharing, ownership of capital by employees, and participative management in business and industry, especially those in which the church has an economic interest. The church should also encourage the formation of low-income, community-controlled economic development enterprises..." (CA-W, 339).

Again, with an eye towards realization and not mere rhetoric, the delegates of the conference appealed to each diocese to establish a commission to monitor the above programs and efforts.

Apostolate and Working Life

Recognizing that the resolutions put forward above will require a foundation, if long-range, enduring results are to be obtained, this recommendation looks toward that objective. To this end, all those involved in ministry should receive "adequate training in Catholic social teaching, economics, social science, and spirituality" (CA-W, 340). Dioceses should officially recognize specialized ministries to working people. Small support groups of people who share a work experience should be formed, for the purpose of prayer, reflection, and constructive action. Catholic educational programs at all levels should reinforce pursuit of the goals mentioned. Catholic scholars should join with others in assessing contemporary economic life, exploring alternatives to the present system, and developing a viable theology of work and leisure. Finally, it is suggested that the USCC stimulate dialogue with labor unions, business organizations, professional societies, and others, "to translate the implications of justice into practical norms of action."

In one sense the interest and enthusiasm surrounding the issues of *Work* did not attract the attention accorded many other sections. On the other hand, the content of the resolutions is possibly the most explosive and far-reaching of the conference in its implications—if acted upon seriously, for it strikes at the very core of current value structures. It is inconceivable that the actions broached can be taken within and outside of the church without conflict and turbulent reactions. To be "poor in spirit" is the first of the beatitudes. It is the beginning of everything——but, it has its price.

Questions for Discussion:

1. Do you think affirmative action programs have any place in the church?
2. Is endorsement of the Equal Rights Amendment a proper action to be taken by a religious entity such as the church?
3. Is it proper for the church to use its financial resources to pressure businesses to adopt policies acceptable within the framework of the church's concept of social justice?
4. What are your feelings about the church's involvement in the unionization of workers, farm laborers, etc.?
5. What specialized ministries to working people seem to be needed in your area?

6. Can you conceive of any alternatives to the "free enterprise system" which would seem more consistent with gospel values?

Issues for Action:

1. Help form a parish economic commission to study the questions raised above and to work for establishment of similar commissions in other parishes and on the diocesan level.
2. Require that your parish/diocese document its efforts to comply with the principles of affirmative action and equal opportunity.
3. Take parish action to assure parish/diocesan accountability for investment practices—in firms which prove their sincere concern for social justice at home and abroad.
4. Design a parish consciousness-raising program to acquaint members with local needs relative to worker representation and collective bargaining.
5. Assign parish funds and personnel to at least one "specialized ministry" on behalf of workers.
6. Plan a forum to bring together various interested and informed parties to discuss the merits of free enterprise and alternatives.

5

Ethnicity and Race

"Blessed are those who mourn, for they shall be
comforted" (Mt.5:4).

Those who mourn because of injustice do so on at
least two counts. There is the pain they suffer because
they are victims. Even more piercing, perhaps, is the
grief weighing them down as they gaze, with awesome
forebearance, upon their church—witnessing the instances in which it too has failed to measure up to the
standards of "liberty and justice *for all.*"

There are the Spanish speaking, who in spite of their
large numbers, are all but powerless in the church.
There are the black Catholics who, even in this consultation process, found their effort to be heard drowned out
by the smallness of their numbers. Yet, when they were
able to speak, "often their testimony consisted of
straightforward statements of faith and experience as
Catholics which were marked by almost incredible cour-
age, persistence, and depth" (WP-E, 8).

There are the native Americans, eloquent in their
witness to "violation of treaty rights, lack of adequate
housing, medical care, and employment opportunity,
and highly discriminatory and destructive educational
programs . . . designed to destroy the distinctive culture
and way of life of Indians" (WP-E, 9). There are the
Lithuanian Catholics, seeking greater support for those

suffering persecution in Iron Curtain countries, and joining with Polish and Italians in an appeal for pastoral care more sensitive to their distinctive linguistic and cultural needs. Finally, there are the Asian-Americans, so easily overlooked and forgotten.

While notable progress has been made, especially in recent years, in overcoming the crimes of the past, racism remains "a cancer not yet exorcised from America" (WP-E,1). Even the church has not been able to liberate itself from its past ambivalence. Whereas in earlier times its generosity on behalf of the poor has been offset by "cruel neglect of those least able to care for themselves," today the tension lies between the conflicting values of unity and diversity. "Catholics often remain prisoners of their own history and their own possessions. They dream of creating an exciting and distinctive American Catholic life and culture, yet, at the same time, of being faithful to their own diversity and pluralism" (WP-E, 3).

The recommendations under *Ethnicity and Race,* then, dissociate themselves from "the melting pot" and the "blaming the victim" perspectives. Uniformity of cultural vision is renounced. Structural as well as personal prejudices come under attack. Racial and ethnic hatred is condemned, not only as a "social problem," but as *sin.* Statements of moral commitment give way to insistence upon decisive action.

Equality in the Church

While the tone of the *Working Paper* was relatively mild and reserved, *Call to Action* delegates chose to denounce Catholic ethnic and racial practices in no uncertain terms. "The teaching of the Catholic church on racial and ethnic equality, together with the ideals of helping the oppressed, is clear. However, the response of the Catholic community in the United States, with certain notable exceptions, is in fact a mockery of this teaching" (CA-E, 333). Resolutions under *Ethnicity and Race,* in contrast, set forth a plan of action which will serve to unite doctrine and life.

An emphatic distinction is drawn between ethnicity and race. The two dimensions involve different (if often parallel) sets of problems. Actions proposed under the present recommendation closely resemble those of *Work.* In the formulation and implementation of church policy, there must be *representation* of racial, ethnic, and cultural groups proportionate to the national makeup of the church. All dioceses should have affirmative action programs, implemented by adequately funded, independent offices—established within one year.

In every aspect of the allocation of its resources the church is mandated to combat racism and discrimination, while also positively promoting justice. Not only should it follow equal opportunity policies in its own hiring and advancement procedures, it should avoid business transactions with firms or institutions which refuse to *take* affirmative action for equal opportunity, and should regularly review its contracts with respect to this norm.

Cultural Pluralism

Church leadership is urged, at all levels, clearly to "assert its commitment to a unity of faith in a pluralism which recognizes and appreciates the right of diverse ethnic, racial and cultural groups to maintain and develop their traditional culture or special interest, such as their distinctive language, customs, and family patterns..." (CA-E, 334). In support of this right, dioceses are asked to help "form or maintain parishes or missions which will give emphasis to certain ethnic, racial, and cultural groups, but are open to providing services for all" (CA-E, 334).

A series of actions leading to a profound appreciation in the church for this kind of pluralism is approved, to include: identification of each parish's composition; relevant training programs for teachers and church leaders; collection and/or preparation of resource materials; establishment of an intercultural materials resource center in each diocese; programs of multicultural education and experience for adults within each parish.

Intense concern is expressed for the future ministry to diverse racial, ethnic, and cultural groups. The latter should be served by priests of their own language and culture. Every effort must be made, therefore, to re-orient seminary training and, indeed, experiment with new training formats in the interim, to encourage entry into the apostolate among black, Hispanic, and other ethnic and racial groups. Equally, there is immediate need for bishops drawn from among these populations. Finally, to foster and accelerate progress on all these fronts, the NCCB should establish a multiethnic office, as well as expand the Spanish-Speaking Secretariat and create a national Hispanic research center.

American Indians

The church is exhorted to set an example by keeping its commitments to native Americans, thereby providing a platform from which the Catholic bishops can call upon this nation and its government to honor its treaties, executive orders, and special agreements. An American Indian secretariat with appropriate native American representation is to be established immediately. The strongest possible attempt should be made to foster and develop American Indian leadership, at all levels, for example, within higher education, seminaries, an Indian diaconate program, the episcopacy, and so on. Educational efforts to favor this development should be pursued both on and off reservations.

Liturgies, both for Indian and non-Indian peoples, should incorporate American Indian traditions, such as the sacred drum, sacred dance, and so on. In general, "the bishops should promote the Indian peoples' prophetic role to deepen and spiritualize the American people through reverse acculturation" (CA-E, 336).

Church Response to Racism and Discrimination

In the *Working Paper* this recommendation addressed only "discrimination" and was comprised of but five resolutions. It was altered by *Call to Action* amendments to include racism in its scope, and was extended to a total of fifteen action proposals, giving some hint of the anguish and depth of feeling accompanying issues in this domain.

The NCCB, working with the various secretariats and offices for minority and ethnic affairs, is to be required to commit itself to national pastoral and social action plans to meet the needs of the communities in question. A task force, with appropriate minority representation, should be assigned by the NCCB to evaluate the work of the Commission for Catholic Missions among the Colored People and the Indians, and the Bureau of Catholic Missions, and to recommend policies.

Research and action should be sponsored by the Campaign for Human Development, for example, to deal with the social and economic needs of urban and rural poor whites. Equal concern is voiced for "the needs of the millions of Appalachian and Puerto Rican migrants" (CA-E, 336).

Most careful consideration should be given to the present educational efforts being made by church agencies on behalf of the groups mentioned, and Asian-American and other ethnic groups as well. High priority should be given to retaining and rendering effective parochial schools already existing in poor urban and rural areas, as a service to the poor on the part of the entire diocese.

The church is not only, through its own agencies, to struggle against racism and discrimination "in such public policy areas as housing, education, neighborhood development and job opportunities, health care and nutrition," it is also urged to cooperate with other agencies in the endeavor—including (but not limited to) ". . . the Anti-Defamation League of B'Nai Brith, the Urban League, the National Association for Advancement of Colored People . . . the National Catholic Conference for Interracial Justice, and Church Women United" (CA-E, 337). The bishops, in particular, are asked to publish a pastoral letter on the sin of racism by April of 1978, for racism is recognized by the delegates as an "evil we must also admit infests the life of the church as well as society" (CA-E, 336).

Other resolutions invoke action to meet an immense

variety of pressing concerns: the alienation of black, Hispanic, and Indian youth from the church; abuse of the press and media to foster discrimination and racism; the need for task forces within each diocese to counteract each instance of racism and discrimination encountered on the local level; establishment of diocesan black, Hispanic, Indian, and ethnic secretariats, and so on.

Ethnicity and Race patently justifies one inference, among many others, namely: racial, ethnic, and cultural minority groups within the Catholic population have reached the limit of endurance. The church must become what it proclaims and do so now. Only a structurally comprehensive approach to the eradication of racism and discrimination will suffice. Church leadership can no longer sit back at a safe and comfortable distance and lament the injustices supposedly being perpetrated only by others. Neither foot-dragging nor half-hearted interminably gradual reform attempts will be tolerated. Through their own painful commitment, those in power must identify with those who mourn for justice, seeking their empowerment. Anything less is unworthy of that body which pretends to be the SIGN of Christ-in-the-world, and will remain incredible and ineffectual.

Questions for Discussion:

1. Have you personally witnessed inconsistencies of Catholic doctrine and practice with regard to respect for racial, ethnic, and cultural diversity?

2. What are the various racial, ethnic, or cultural groups identifiable in your parish/diocese?
3. Can you identify ways in which the riches of racial, ethnic, and cultural diversity could be better tapped by your parish/diocese?
4. What are your feelings about the obligations of your parish/diocese and the national church toward native Americans?
5. How have you experienced racism in your life; what have you done about it?
6. What do you feel are the causes of alienation from the church on the part of *youth* from the groups mentioned?

Issues for Action:

1. Plan a parish reconciliation service, uniting a detailed confession of sins of racism and discrimination with a celebration stressing racial, ethnic, and cultural values.
2. Sponsor a parish/diocesan study to determine racial, ethnic, and cultural composition and needs in your area.
3. Design a special forum, involving native Americans, to acquaint your parish with their needs and to explore avenues of interaction.
4. Create a parish commission for promotion of racial, ethnic, and cultural justice, and to counteract instances of racism and discrimination in your locality.
5. Acquaint parish members with programs carried out through the Campaign for Human Development and sponsor a program to raise funds for the latter. Study the feasibility of submitting a project for funding.

6. With parish youth initiate a program to bring together young people from various minorities to propose plans to render the parish more responsive to their needs and aspirations.

6

Personhood

"Blessed are the pure of heart, for they shall see God" (Mt. 5:8).

Who, indeed, are the "pure of heart"? Those, one would think, who are so single-minded in their pursuit of the goals set forth for us by the gospel that they are able to cut through even the unparalleled muddle of values clouding our times. Those who, in the simplicity and authenticity of their unselfishness, are transparent to Christ and he to them, in the power of the Spirit. In other words, "the pure of heart" represents a reality that we are not, whether church or individual, but which Christian love summons us to become.

The difficulty of the challenge is eloquently described in the *Working Paper* on *Personhood*. As in *Ethnicity and Race* the aspiration for social justice embraced the task of resolving the tension between diversity and unity with regard to racial, ethnic, and cultural uniqueness, here an analogous tension appears, now at the level of the individual person in face of the community. The clarity of vision, genuineness, and freedom from ulterior motives called for is that which will enable the church, as a community of persons, to find the narrow gate that opens between excessive individualism, on the one side, and the rigidity of an inflexible societal framework on the other.

"Papal social teaching, prior to Vatican II . . ." it is observed, "tended to emphasize human dignity within ordered community and to underestimate the importance of personal freedom." In recent years the church has come to "a more positive understanding of the value of personal freedom." Human dignity is correlative to freedom. "Freedom is the catalyst needed if the dignity of the person is to be real." Freedom that is not merely independence from external controls, but responsible freedom, freedom from sin, freedom fully to develop one's own unique potential, freedom really to live one's own life and make one's own choices, in reciprocity with the obligation to respect the rights of others and to contribute to the well-being of society (WP-P, 2).

The church's commitment to freedom interpreted in this sense, moreover, must become more than an abstract principle. It must be reflected in actual pastoral practice. The following recommendations ensuing from the two years of consultation and the Detroit conference provide a demanding, if tentative, agenda for action which will assure progress toward the genre of freedom that defines true actualization of human persons in their full potential—albeit with their sinfulness, and weaknesses, and need for reconciliation as well.

Christian Community

Almost paradoxically, the initial emphasis of *Personhood* is on building community, in the awareness that individuals cannot become themselves in isolation from others. The NCCB is asked to give priority to development of community, particulary at the parish level.

"Church movements which unite persons in small communities in worship, prayer, study, evangelization and apostolic service should be affirmed and encouraged" (CA-P, 1). In brief, personal growth needs to be grounded firmly in communal spirituality.

Call to Action delegates unequivocally assert the importance and equality in dignity of each vocation "as a divine call to a specific way to witness the life of Christ." Every Christian community is asked to value the gifts of individuals for service, and the NCCB is urged "to reconsider policies and church structures that exclude persons from ministry. . . ." The resource base for the office of preaching should be broadened to invite the contributions of women and youth, as well as unordained men, married couples, and laicized priests. The assumption seems to be that the individual Christian lives of all can be enriched in the measure that the individual gifts and talents of all are utilized to the maximum (CA-P, 314).

Personal Development

The church as a personal associate of individuals with personal needs is envisioned here. In keeping with a focus of concern characterizing the entire consultation, the greatest stress is placed upon the responsibility of the church to reach out more effectively to the aging. The latter must be recognized as a resource (and not a liability) to the church, above all in the quality of their spirituality, oriented as it is toward contemplation—a dimension so typically suppressed in the rush of our times. At the same time the church should both provide programs needed by the aging, and function as an advocate for their rights " in the areas of housing, health, employment, transportation, and economics" (CA-P, 315).

A strong plea is made for the rights of the unborn, as the 1975 Bishops' Pastoral Plan for Pro-Life Activities is endorsed. The need to eliminate all discrimination based on sex, and to struggle for full recognition of the equal dignity and rights of women is once more asserted and the ERA again endorsed.

Attention is dramatically called to the problem of alienation of young people from the church. Parishes and dioceses are asked to develop ministries for youth between 13 and 18, and even more particularly for young adults in the 18 to 35 age range. Programs should "foster the total personal and spiritual growth of each young person," and pastoral plans should be initiated, implemented, and subjected to ongoing evaluation by the bishops, in collaboration with young people.

Other social concerns treated elsewhere in the conference are also considered under *Personhood,* but for the sake of conciseness will not be discussed. The needs of two frequently slighted groups, namely the handicapped and those subjected to the criminal justice system (also to be considered under *Nationhood*), however, will receive repeated reflection.

The value to the church of the unique gifts of handicapped persons is affirmed. Yet, it is suggested that the church regularly fails to include such individuals on an equal basis. As with the aging, here too the church should both strive to provide needed programs itself, and advocate "the principle of normalization so that the handicapped can find housing, employment, social life, educational opportunities, and valuable spiritual and parish life" (CA-P, 315).

Educational programs should be offered to raise general awareness (of clergy and laity alike) of the talents and needs of the handicapped. A feasibility study should be sponsored by the NCCB/USCC with regard to establishment of a national Catholic office for the handicapped, thereby institutionalizing systematic pursuit of the interests of this group.

With respect to prisoners, the church advocates their entitlement to rights as human beings and to full human development. To implement this principle, the delegates insist upon extension of civil rights to all prisoners, organized efforts to replace prisons by community alternatives, abolition of capital punishment, development of parish outreach programs to facilitate reentry, and prevention of involvement of teenagers in the criminal justice system, for example, through elimination of "so-called status offenses" (CA-P, 316).

It is perhaps noteworthy that in the *Working Paper* this recommendation was limited to six resolutions. Not only were three resolutions added through amendments (including that respecting prisoners), the necessity of meeting a deadline for termination of the Detroit assembly resulted in the tabling of seventeen additional amendments—much to the chagrin of the delegates of that working committee. The urgency with which the church is summoned to help lead the way for the full personal development of all, therefore, is unmistakably and poignantly impressive.

Sexuality

Though it is undoubtedly unwarranted to identify the "pure of heart" with those whose life is sexually blameless, the proper integration of one's sexuality is vital to personal development, as well as to the soundness of marital and family life. To become pure of heart includes the struggle to achieve this integration on the part of individuals, couples, and the Christian community as a whole. Resolutions under this recommendation point to the necessary conditions, if such genuine integration is to be even a possibility.

Here too the tension between a consistency of viewpoint and diversity of values is evident. While commitment to "the validity of personal sexual fulfillment in married life" is fundamental, it also serves as a reference point for dialogue with others "who are expressing their sexuality in a variety of life styles. . . ." "Such dialogue should be conducted with respect for the dignity, freedom, and responsibility of each person, and should incorporate reflection on human experience and gospel values, as well as on Christian tradition and church teaching" (CA-P, 316).

Ultimately, the values which guide real personal actualization and genuine community must reinforce one another. In the complexity of modern life, however, it is not without ambiguity that we seek to differentiate such values from others which are based either on individual indulgence or institutional self-interest and illusory righteousness. In the process, it is adequate pastoral care and the pursuit of informed consciences that become realistic objectives. That is, the emphasis is not on "purity of doctrine," but on actual caring for persons caught up in the painfulness of the dilemmas inevitably presented by life itself, taking due account of the experience of those who live the problems being addressed.

Thus, with regard to contraception, bishops are pressed to act pastorally, "to affirm more clearly the right and responsibility of married people to form their own consciences...." The involved nature of the question of birth control and family planning is not underestimated. All input, from *Humanae Vitae* to the "spiritual and emotional quality" of marital and family lives, is to be weighed in the balance. Still, the final responsibility is said to lie with married people, in the counsel of their own decision of conscience.

Again, respecting the difficult challenge that mature sexuality offers, *Call to Action* reflects on the need for refinement of educational approaches. Not only should such programs begin for the young at an early age, effective programs should also be designed and made available to parents—as those who have primary responsibility for the education of their children in sexual matters.

Understanding for minorities, this time in the sexual realm, is once more demonstrated. Whatever we might think about the morality of homosexual acts, the church has a responsibility to serve the pastoral needs of those with a homosexual orientation. It should also join in advocating respect for their basic constitutional rights, including the right to be free from discrimination against them as persons. In support of this notion, delegates voted that the church extend official recognition to DIGNITY, a Catholic organization serving the needs of those of homosexual orientation.

A Catholic Bill of Rights

In the interest of "purification of her own life" and defense of the rights of the baptized, the church is asked to prepare a *Bill of Rights* for U.S. Catholics, ultimately to be included within canon law. Therein the church's commitment both to fundamental and procedural rights (due process) would be institutionalized concretely. Included among others would be: "the right to freedom of conscience, freedom of speech, freedom of assembly, and freedom to participate, in accord with each person's gift of the Spirit in the life and ministry of the Christian Community on a non-discriminatory basis . . ." (CA-P, 317).

Whereas it was the task of the *Call to Action* consultation to bring to the surface the aspirations and priority needs of the people of the U.S. Catholic church, as expressed by the people themselves, and not to revise church doctrine, the process has made it increasingly apparent that if the church is to grow in healthy unity and credibility, it must somehow achieve a higher level of congruence, bringing official teaching and pastoral guidance into closer correlation with the practice of committed Christians. Time limitations made full discussion of the above proposals impossible. It cannot be concluded, then, that in their specificity they represent a consensus of the faithful. In their basic orientation, however, they are consistent with two years of testimony, and deserve to be heeded as a cry for a unified effort promoting human development, that together we might move toward the ideal of becoming, in fact, pure of heart.

Questions for Discussion:

1. In what ways has your parish life made you feel alone? How has it given you a sense of mutual support?
2. Do you believe all vocations are equal, or do some possess greater dignity than others?
3. Does your parish find in its aging a valuable resource? Does it have a program of outreach to the elderly?
4. Do young people, ages thirteen to thirty-five, play an active role in your parish? How could this role be further developed?
5. How do the people in your parish feel and act about questions of personal freedom and development, family planning, and abortion?
6. What do you feel are the obligations of a parish toward such groups as the handicapped, those of homosexual orientation, prisoners, and former offenders?

Issues for Action:

1. Design a pilot program to test the feasibility of developing a variety of small "support groups" within the parish.
2. Assign a task force to study and contribute to parish

education in the matter of the dignity of all vocations. Consider vocational counseling as an appropriate parish service.

3. Prepare a liturgical celebration accenting the dignity and value of the aging, and focusing on parish efforts to meet their needs. Join with other groups or agencies to identify and serve unmet needs, e.g., through congregate feeding.

4. Study each facet of the parish system, with the aim of increasing the participation and authority vested in the young.

5. Evaluate the parish/diocese's sex education program—for parents as well as children. Study means of improving it, in terms of education for life and not merely sex.

6. Engage a representative committee in drawing up a constitution or bill of rights pertinent to your parish.

7

Nationhood

"Blessed are the peacemakers, for they shall be called the children of God" (Mt. 5:9).

Acting effectively as a peacemaker has little to do with avoidance of tension. On the contrary, achievement of peace, the harmony that accompanies a state of justice, presupposes constant willingness to engage in the conflict necessary to alter those conditions which inevitably lead to violence and warfare. Serenity, characteristically, is rare in the struggle for peace.

In extending its vision from internal affairs of the church to public issues critical to the nation's well-being, then, *Call to Action* does not back off from the challenges and controversy inherent in interaction between church and state, in order to progress in the direction of a nation-at-peace. While at times it is proper for the church to express itself on behalf of national unity, the *Working Paper* on *Nationhood* argues, in many instances a critical, prophetic stance should be assumed, "measuring national life and public action by the standards of the gospel." ". . . The sometimes conflicting demands of conscience and civic policies must be worked out in the ongoing dialogue between church and nation. Whether this dialogue takes place in the public arena of politics or within the church community, its vigorous pursuit is indispensable to the formation of the moral consicence of the nation" (WP-NA, 1-2).

Three guiding principles are identified which orient the church in its efforts to contribute to the formation of public conscience on issues of public policy: "the transcendent value of the human person, the duty of the state to serve the common good, and the principle of subsidiarity" (WP-NA, 2).

Subsidiarity is especially stressed, as crucial to the maintenance of a nation of responsible persons. It "encourages individuals and communities to exercise their own freedom for actions that they judge to be valuable" (WP-NA, 10). More than this, however, subsidiarity favors prudent decentralization and resists uncritical acceptance of federal government intervention. It is not a question simply of freedom, but of corresponding responsibility, the responsibility to take action to solve problems at the local community level, whenever possible.

The data of the consultation revealed parishes and dioceses as primarily concerned with the culture of the nation, for example, prevalence of materialistic values. Witnesses in the hearings, on the other hand, directed attention to the structures and institutions dominating public life. All in all, a balanced, moderate appeal was issued for reordering of national priorities, in light of the fact that our present system, through its laws and economic mechanisms, disproportionately burdens the young, the poor, the nonwhite, the unfortunate, the unconventional, the noncitizen, the rebel, the prisoner (WP-NA, 7).

The consultation process, moreover, reveals "an honest consistency between actions recommended for the larger society and for the church itself. Thus, opposition to materialism in society is matched with a call for simpler life styles among lay, religious, and clerical Catholics. Concern for the poor is matched by a recommendation to share church resources with the poor . . ." (WP-NA, 8).

The "call" in *Call to Action,* nonetheless, is not merely for church leaders to speak courageously. All Catholics are expected "to provide prophetic witness to the nation." Always there will be disagreement about which specific policies are to be followed. Still, pseudo-pluralism is intolerable, that is, the "pluralism that excludes the weak and powerless," serving "not the common good, but those who benefit from the weaknesses of others." The church, in its own unity-through-diversity, is uniquely equipped to expose such injustice, and to foster a healthy pluralism. It cannot do so, however, without risk to its own equanimity. "What most witnesses begged for, and what some witnesses predicted would never happen, was a bicentennial resolution for action—specific, public, far-reaching, even dangerous" (WP-NA, 10–11). The subsequent recommendations embody that hope.

Political Responsibility

The entire church has a responsibility to strive to increase the impact of Christian witness and values upon public policy, to venture to exercise prophetic influence.

Since the political arena is one of extreme intricacy, the necessary foundation for measured intervention must be laid. Hence, parishes, dioceses, and so on, must provide education encompassing the relationship between the gospel and public policy, the duties of citizenship, and the way public policy is made.

Committees for political responsibility, composed primarily of lay people and representatives of the poor and powerless, should be established at all levels of church life, especially for the purpose of defining issues and setting priorities for public policy.

In brief, beyond "ad hoc" educational efforts, the church must commit itself to a structural approach, ensuring systematic, comprehensive, and consistent effort to confront public policy makers with evangelical demands.

Goals for Public Policy

Conference delegates insist upon response to the need for a reordering of national priorities through fifteen relatively specific action resolutions. Some resolutions reiterate proposals considered elsewhere and need not be repeated. Others are new, or add a new measure of emphasis.

The nation is urged to adopt a policy of peace, including more serious steps toward disarmament, above all in order to free resources indispensable for meeting basic social needs. A national policy essentially rejecting abortion is advocated. The problem of crime receives extensive attention. Elimination of poverty and racism are interpreted as the most effective means of reducing crime. Additional policy objectives include humanization of the penal system and just compensation to victims of crime.

A national policy of income security for all is supported. A system of taxation shifting the burden to those most able to pay is called for. A plan for comprehensive health care should be provided. Decent housing at reasonable cost should be available to all Americans. Exploitative ownership and speculation in land must be ended.

Concrete steps toward a foreign policy more authentically responsive to the human rights and dignity of all peoples are enumerated: denying all forms of aid to countries "violating internationally recognized standards of human and civil rights"; international commodity price agreements; opening U.S. markets to Third and Fourth World exports; a code of behavior for U.S. multinational corporations (CA-NA, 331).

In addition to other resolutions which again call for equal treatment and rejection of all forms of discrimination, a final proposal invites reform of public assistance, to render it more adequate to meet the needs of the poor, for example, by better national coordination, and through community self-help programs.

Morality and Public Policy

The moral issues raised here are, for the most part, an item for item reflection of the public policy goals enunciated above. Special attention is devoted, however, to two national "institutions" of critical significance: our economic system itself, and the mass media sustaining it.

Delegates assert "that many of the basic values of our present economic system appear to be directly in conflict with gospel values. . . ." Aside from the materialistic orientation of excessive consumerism, the values in question are not named. Generically they are identified as those economic forces bearing a causal relationship to the social ills we observe around us. It is recommended, then, "that the church support research exploring alternative and innovate economic structures that will distribute power more equitably" (CA-NA, 332).

As for the media, Catholic agencies are asked to join with other coalitions to influence network and local programming and advertising in the direction of greater human and aesthetic quality. More specifically, dehumanizing values and excessive consumerism must be counteracted; access to the media on behalf of public interests should be assured; positive programming and advertising characterized by human aesthetic quality should be promoted. In this regard, the bishops are asked not only to lend verbal support, but to dedicate resources to the endeavor.

Ongoing Implementation

While there were many types of self-interest and differences of viewpoint distinguishing participants in the *Call to Action* consultation, all seemed to unite in their conviction that the process itself was eminently valuable, and in their concern about what would follow after the conference ended. The desire was voiced, therefore, and overwhelmingly approved, for a structure to be responsible for implementation.

It was resolved that the process of consultation, with emphasis on participative decisionmaking, should become a regular element in the national life of the U.S.

Catholic church, and be extended through local structures to diocesan and parish levels. Even more to the point, the NCCB was entreated to establish a racially, ethnically, and culturally representative task force from among the delegates, to work with the bishops on the mandate for implementation, and to plan for a subsequent consultation in five years to evaluate the efforts of the previous period, and to extend the project still further into the future. Adequate resources, it is made explicit, should be allocated to assure and to reinforce implementation of *Call to Action* at all levels, whether national, regional, diocesan, or parish.

Finally, all delegates committed themselves "to promote the implementation of the recommendations of this conference" (CA-NA, 332).

If there is a prevailing value throughout *Nationhood*, it is the sacredness of all life, whether that of the woman subjected to discrimination, that of the unborn child, that of the soldier, or that of the criminal on death row. In cognizance of the almost omnipresent threat to life itself, as well as to the values underlying quality of life, *Call to Action* advocates a new and daring openness, in which the quest for peace becomes a search for a socioeconomic, political, cultural system in which the irradicable dignity of *all* persons, and not the comfort of even the top 80 percent, is of foremost concern.

Depending on the quality of "follow-up" efforts, the Catholic church in the U.S., if the energy and dedication typifying the *Call to Action* consultation is a valid witness, is approaching an unprecedented moment of opportunity to make a difference, not only in the lives of Catholics, but of all U.S. citizens, of all brothers and sisters interdependent with us across the planet earth. Through the voices of the "grassroots," those suffering and longing for justice, the Lord has once more spoken, setting before the church as he once did before Moses and his people "life and good, death and evil." The bishops of the United States carry on their shoulders an unenviable burden. While we all have our part to play, ultimately, as did Moses for his people, as did the apostles for theirs, they must and will largely decide the fate of Catholicism for our time. The hopes of all, in the final analysis, rest upon these few men and their judgment, their capacity to recognize what is good, to discern the truth, to choose life—that all may live, that together we may harvest peace, in the one family of the children of God (cf. Dt. 30:15-20).

Questions for Discussion:

1. What steps do you think the parish/diocese should take to simplify its life style? How can you moderate your own "consumerism?"
2. How do you think important policies are really decided—in the church? In the public sector?
3. What personal "power" would you be willing to surrender so that others less fortunate than yourself might increase the power they exercise over their destiny?
4. Do you believe our penal systems should become more human, and that capital punishment should be abolished? What are the penal facilities in your area like?

5. Would you favor a national policy of basic income security for all? Why or why not?
6. What aspects of the "welfare system" do you think are most in need of reform? What types of people are recipients of welfare aid?

Issues for Action:

1. Launch a parish effort to restrict consumerism (goods, energy, etc.) over a specified period of time. Set aside the funds saved and devote them to a stated purpose.
2. Select a specific public and/or church policy as a target, and organize a parish effort to influence its development.
3. Create a parish commission to work towards the "transfer of power" to disadvantaged groups in your neighborhood or region.
4. Work together with officials of a regional penal system to facilitate "reentry" of inmates after they are released.
5. Design a forum utilizing experts on the welfare system, income security, comprehensive health plans, etc.
6. Establish a parish mechanism to contact diocesan and national officials periodically to ascertain the progress being made on implementation of *A Call to Action.*

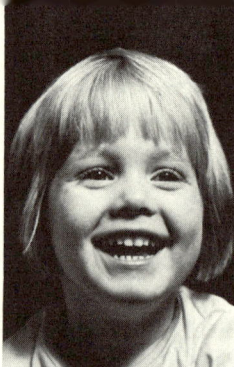

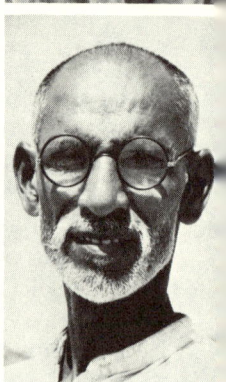

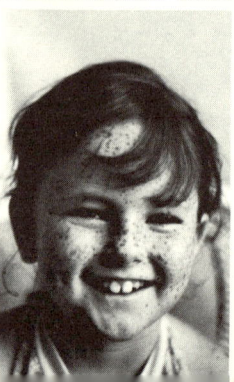

8

Humankind

"Blessed are the meek, for they shall inherit the earth" (Mt. 5:5).

In the final section of *A Call to Action* it is in the spirit of the meekness of the beatitudes that we witness the concern for life and the quest for peace expressed under *Nationhood* extended to embrace the universal family of *Humankind,* in recognition of the interdependence of all individuals and all peoples.

"Meekness," in Western culture at least, has acquired for itself a bad name. It conjures up the image of docile acceptance of exploitation and abuse. The meekness of the gospel, and of the *Call to Action* consultation, on the contrary, constitutes the guiding force of a kind of evangelical imperialism, the outrageous ambition to conquer the world—with love, not defense budgets.

It would be misleading, however, to claim that an attitude of universal meekness, that is, sensitivity to the humanness of others, regardless of national identity, characterizes the majority of U.S. Catholics, or indeed the delegates to *Call to Action.* In comparison to other priorities, the requirements of global justice rated low on the scale even of the Detroit conference. Those who participated in the *Humankind* section were as intense as others in their eagerness for justice—but their concerns were those of a decided minority. The vision of others, while piercing, was more narrow in scope. As the *Working Paper* on *Humankind* phrases it, "The consciousness of the American Catholic people on the subject of global community . . . is not as sharp as that on the topics of neighborhood or church" (WP-H, 1).

The problem, however, is that as far as most Catholics are concerned, such leadership does not seem to have been compelling. Why? The reasons are diverse but mutually reinforcing. The overwhelming dimensions of world issues and resulting complexity of potential solutions intimidate; physical and cultural distance from the areas where the suffering is most severe tend to render the problems of others remote, if not almost totally "unreal" to our consciousness; the hostility of many elements in "foreign" nations toward the U.S. makes it easy to label others as enemies or competitors, rather than brothers and sisters in the human family; even if we wish to act to bring about change, what possible causal relationship can there be between the minor adjustments we can make in our life style, and the immense needs of developing nations? Lastly, as we have seen in the other sections of the conference, the scope and depth of needs "at home" are so vast and urgent that the relationship of these needs to international factors becomes difficult, if not impossible, to grasp. Given these very considerable forces bolstering psychological resistance to any message which might contradict such assumptions, the educational efforts on the papal and episcopal levels to communicate the imperatives of global justice, though extensive, have remained comparatively feeble, both in the technique and the impact of the communication.

Be this as it may, not only contemporary church teaching, but secular experience as well, dictate that continuation of our myopia portends disaster not only for poor nations, but for ourselves as well—with or without the benefit of a nuclear conflagration. Even now we persist in manufacturing and purchasing illusions of security (overly spacious homes, luxury automobiles, and so on), while we close our schools, displace workers because of lack of energy to operate our industries, and on and on. Thus the fruits of the assertiveness of desire! It is no longer the infants of Calcutta starving in the alleys. Now it is our own children frost-bitten, our aged frozen—as fuel runs low and heat is cut off. The United States, some 6 percent of the world's population, annually continues to consume 30 to 40 percent of its production. Our brothers in Chile and sisters in the Philippines have never been able to afford our extravagance. Now, not even we can manage.

The *Call to Action* delegation comprising *Humankind*, therefore, has postulated the end to our illusions and outlined steps toward a new order. In a preamble the participants acknowledge "with gratitude all the positive elements in our heritage," but equally affirm "our complicity in the many injustices committed at home and abroad through our uncritical acceptance of the social, economic, and political system in which we participate." Action on the following recommendations is urged as the only adequate way to give proof that we do "hear the cries of our oppressed brothers and sisters," that our solidarity with them is generated by meekness, the loving embrace of Christ, and not merely by an expediency forced upon us by our childish fantasies, selfishness, and waste (CA-H, 325).

Education for Global Justice

Meaningful, effective action must be preceded by intensive analysis and prayerful reflection, that is, it must be based on consciousness that is not only "aware," but is sophisticated in its grasp of the problems at hand, and inspired by the wisdom that derives from grace alone. The present recommendation, therefore, summons the church to a new level of "education for global justice," accurately informed in its data and firmly grounded in its spirituality.

The approach described is institutional and comprehensive. By June, 1978, each diocese is to have an office for justice and peace. These offices will be assisted by a strengthened office of International Justice & Peace at the national level. Through the latter, moreover, the USCC is asked to "maintain in New York an office with professional staff as a center of information and liaison with the United Nations headquarters," as well as to establish "an official representation with the National Council of Churches," and "enter into dialogue with other world religions on the issues of justice and peace" (CA-H, 327).

In recognition of the inefficacy of present methods of education and communication, a series of resolutions proposes more creative and imaginative endeavors. Research groups should be tasked with designing and testing new models of justice education; other research centers are envisioned to learn more about the important variables governing socio-economic justice, in order better to be able to explore alternative systems. Other traditions (for example, socialist, Ghandian) are to be examined for possible relevance to contemporary situations.

Current knowledge, refined through subsequent research, is to be incorporated into workshops and training programs for all engaged in the educational enterprise—whether bishops in their leadership role, or clergy and laity in their supportive functions. Educational programs should then be implemented throughout the church, addressed to the whole person, including experiential as well as theoretical elements, and respecting the principle of lifelong learning (that is, educate adults as adults, not children).

The effect of such programs is to be enhanced by careful attention to the techniques and personnel utilized in the communication effort. Bishops are asked regularly to turn a critical eye on the effectiveness of their own communications, among themselves and with the people of the church. Those experienced in the needs of the Third and Fourth Worlds, for example, both indigenous representatives and returning missionaries, are to be more widely engaged in the consciousness-raising effort. The church is advised to make more extensive use of the press, radio, and television, to project a "more comprehensive view of global justice before the public."

The symbolical and practical value of "small intentional communities" such as Catholic Worker is to be recognized and promoted. For, in fact, these "have also proven to be first-line outreach to the orphan, widow, and the stranger in the land at a time when we have more and more people sleeping in the streets and refugees coming from other countries" (CA-H, 328).

(The reference to the Catholic Worker is not without irony. At the very moment *A Call to Action* representatives were approving this "small intentional community" in principle and denouncing the arms race, outside of the Detroit assembly hall the local police were arresting Catholic Worker members for demonstrating against the Trident submarine. The gap between the aspirations of the documents under review and the stubbornness of the actualities we face could not be more unambiguously exposed.)

Defense of Human Rights

Education for global justice must be accompanied, not simply followed ("someday") by action. Here various levels of action are proposed. The USCC and NCCB are pressed to lead the Catholic community in full use of the power and resources at its disposal on behalf of the universal defense of human rights. Pressure should be brought on agencies of governments to withhold military or economic aid to governments displaying "a pattern of gross violations of human rights." Corporate involvement in such nations should be restricted. Not only verbal but economic pressure should be brought to bear, as Catholics and their institutions are commissioned to review their investment, with a view toward divestment if the corporations in question are not responsive (CA-H, 328).

Also on the institutional level, identification with "the defense of human rights as stipulated in the UN Universal Declaration of Human Rights" (the right of self-determination in particular) is asserted, and ratification of "the UN Covenants on Civil and Political Rights and Social and Economic Rights" by the U.S. government is advocated. At the same time, areas where parish and/or individual commitment can be evidenced are outlined: continued implementation of the Bishops' Pastoral Plan on the world food crisis; inclusion of Operation Rice Bowl as a regular part of Lenten observance; enrollment of parishes and individuals in the Christian lobbying group on matters related to world hunger; Bread for the World; increasing our sense of moral responsibility to share the world's goods; and simplification of our life style through reduction of unnecessary consumption.

Other organizational efforts recommended include evaluation of the activities of Catholic Relief Services, in order to render it "an even more effective instrument for the integral development of people . . . ," church action to bring to a halt the various abuses of undocumented immigrants, and similar efforts to awaken both national and international consciousness to the situation of political prisoners under repressive governments, as well as to the "continuing suppression of the religious, political, cultural, and other human rights of the oppressed nations of Eastern Europe . . ." (CA-H, 329).

Disarmament and Peace

It is perhaps in the final recommendation of this culminating section of *A Call to Action* that we meet the clearest expression of the meekness to which we are summoned in the sermon on the mount, the utopianism to which we are invited by our heritage and our faith.

The recommendation begins with a recapitulation of biblical, papal, and episcopal teaching. Isaiah 2:4 would have us beat our swords into plowshares, our spears into pruning hooks. For Matthew it is the small matter of being perfect as our heavenly Father is perfect, loving rather than hating our enemies, praying for our persecutors (Mt. 5:44,48). John XXIII in *Pacem in Terris* fills in the details of the imperative of meekness for our times:

> Justice, then, right reason and consideration for human dignity and life urgently demand that the arms race should cease; that the stockpiles which exist in various countries should be reduced equally and simultaneously by the parties concerned; that nuclear weapons should be banned; and finally that all come to an agreement on a fitting program of disarmament, employing mutual and effective controls (Quoted in CA-H, 329).

More recent statements of the magisterium have been even more absolute. The bishops at Vatican II unreservedly condemned acts of war "aimed indiscriminately at the destruction of entire cities and of extensive areas along with their population." Cardinal John Krol, representing the U.S. hierarchy in 1971, called for reversal of current directions of the arms race. Pope Paul VI has insisted on the banning of atomic weapons, and the outlawing of manufacture, proliferation, and storing of such weapons. His statement of the Holy See to the UN in 1976 comments that "the waste involved in the overproduction of military devices," especially given the vital needs that go unsatisfied in developing countries and among the poor and marginal in affluent societies, "*is in itself an act of aggression* against those who are the victims of it. It is an act of aggression which amounts to a crime, for *even when they are not used,* by their cost alone *armaments kill the poor by causing them to starve"* (CA-H, 330).

The resolutions of *A Call to Action,* as radical as they may seem, are but the logical extension of the above teaching. It is recommended that the U.S. Catholic community not merely speak out, but actively resist "the production, possession, proliferation, and threatened use of nuclear weapons and all other weapons of indiscriminate effect. . . ." Nuclear materials convertible to military or terrorist purposes must be carefully controlled. The sale or transfer of arms overseas should be halted. Efforts towards reconciliation and economic development assistance should displace the arming of potential combatants. The U.S. itself must convert to a peace-based economy, as more consistent with the human needs of the world, and to reduce the economic pressures flowing from the dynamics of a defense economy.

The bishops of the U.S. are to exercise leadership in a moral reorientation of the church and its people toward these objectives. These endeavors should be extended through educational programs which "include the search for non-violent alternatives to national defense," programs which explore Pope Paul's theme for the 1977 World Day of Peace, "If you want peace, defend life" (CA-H, 330).

Specific attitudes and actions for peace recommended by the conference include a generous amnesty (much more encompassing than that recently granted by President Carter) for those affected by questions of military service during the Vietnam War, pressure for full disclosure of information relative to prisoners of war and the missing in action, exploration of forms of ministry alternative to the current system of military chaplaincy, and support of movements for justice and freedom in other nations ("South Africa, Chile, those countries under Communist domination, Korea, the Philippines, Northern Ireland, and Lebanon, to name a few.") through nonviolent material and spiritual assistance (CA-H, 330).

A final resolution of the conference with regard to arms and peace calls to mind a disclaimer once issued by the apostle, Paul. "So it is that neither he who plants nor he who waters is anything, but only God who gives the growth" (1 Cor. 3:7). Peace, the fostering of life, ultimately finds its foundation not in material fortresses, nor even in humanistic declarations, but in spiritual energy. *A Call to Action,* therefore, sets forth the need for services of reconciliation between peoples and nations, "so that the world community can face in prayer the fact that large numbers of people have already perished through the use of indiscriminate weaponry" (CA-H, 330).

The cynic may well wonder, "How does one arrange a reconciliation service with the Russians?" The Christian believer can only meekly reply, "Historically, the eventual outcome of proliferation of armaments is depressingly predictable. The gifts of the Spirit are not." No doubt the resolutions summarized above have about them a certain guilelessness. But then, to paraphrase and expand upon one delegate's articulation of his feelings on the matter, "In this country there are innumerable forces pressing for more arms, for higher defense expenditures. If the church cannot take an unequivocal stand on the side of disarmament, then who shall? Who will be the voice of the Prince of Peace among the nations of the earth?"

Questions for Discussion:

1. What efforts have been made in your parish to familiarize its members with the church's teaching on global justice?
2. How can your parish/diocese cooperate with other churches or secular groups in addressing the needs of people in developing nations?
3. What is the significance of *experiential* learning with regard to problems of global justice?
4. How do you feel about efforts of the U.S. to aid other countries financially and militarily?
5. Do you favor U.S. ratification of UN covenants on civil, political, social and economic rights?
6. How far do you believe the U.S. should go in taking the initiative toward disarmament? What are the risks if we do? What are the dangers if we do not?

Issues for Action:

1. Organize a series of study/action groups with the task of raising the parish's consciousness of the implications of current church doctrine on global justice.
2. Form a parish commission to contact other groups, with the goal of creating a coalition to enter into direct interaction with individuals and/or groups in a Third or Fourth World nation.

3. Design a workshop emphasizing the use of *experiential* learning, with the objective of increasing sensitivity to the needs of developing peoples.

4. Sponsor a forum bringing together legislators and other policy-makers to discuss the merits of current U.S. foreign policy. Seek support, in particular, for the establishment and maintenance of a world food reserve.

5. Invite experts in UN affairs to inform your parish about UN activities, especially the covenants pending ratification.

6. Generate a coalition to influence your diocese to carry out one or more demonstrations in opposition to the arms race and current handling of nuclear materials. Use the occasion to explore nonviolent means of national defense.

Conclusion

While members of the hierarchy can and have engaged in individual initiatives, and while priests, religious and laity, particularly those in positions of influence, can accomplish a great deal, the destiny of *A Call to Action* lies ultimately in the collective heart, mind, and intestinal fortitude of the bishops of the United States. Whether the potential of the consultation is fulfilled, or it becomes just another series of meetings, depends on the amount of legitimacy the NCCB/USCC is willing to grant that the process possessed. To that degree the bishops will take systematic action on the recommendations reviewed.

A number of criticisms of the legitimacy of the process have been formulated, many by some of the bishops themselves. It has been contended that the Detroit assembly was not representative, that it was composed of a biased selection of delegates and manipulated by powerful lobbying groups. It was, therefore, controlled by the "liberal wing" of the church. The resolutions issuing from *A Call to Action,* moreover, were not only the fruit of liberals; for a variety of reasons they are too impractical and unrealistic to implement. In many cases the resolutions exceed the capacity of the church's personnel and funds. Even if they could be acted upon, the result would be an incredibly huge, complex, unmanageable bureaucracy. In other instances, though the actions proposed may be feasible, they are ill-founded in light of the church's doctrine and law. In sum, lack of balanced representation and thorough discussion resulted in a hodgepodge of proposals of doubtful merit, hardly the kind of solid substance of which a five year plan might be composed.

Advocates of the validity of *A Call to Action,* on the other hand, while conceding that a venture of so immense a scale necessarily will have shortcomings, are far from mute in response to the criticisms compiled. There is good reason to believe that the consultation process, taken as a whole, was indeed representative of what it was supposed to represent: the needs of humankind. Probably it is true that those who participated most actively were more typical of professional and highly committed Catholics than of the average parishioner, but is it not from just this kind of population that leaders should seek consultation in order to plan for the future?

Again, it is accurate that lobbying groups did have an impact—but only on a small percentage of the 218 resolutions eventually approved. Secondly, the resolutions they affected, for example, ordination of women, disarmament, and so on, had already emerged from the two years of consultation and were present, in essence, in the *Working Papers.* The chief effect of the "vested interests" was to place these issues more squarely before the consciousness of the conference, and somewhat to radicalize their content. Still, this impact hardly amounts to domination of the conference by "liberals." One can point to many "conservative" proposals supported by the delegates with equal fervor, for example, renewal of rural life, encouragement of vocations to the priesthood, condemnation of abortion, and tax support for private schools.

As for the challenge of impracticality, it must be accepted quite seriously. The division of the Detroit conference into eight sections and numerous subsections, without time being available for coordination, inevitably led to suggestions for new structures and uses of personnel which duplicated one another, or at least overlapped. In this respect, however, the issue is not the proliferation of structures, but the principle of structural reform—in line with the values inspiring the recommendations. The church and its leadership are expected to do, not the impossible, but what is realistic—within the guidelines of new priorities and a more keen set of insights.

Undoubtedly it is also to be acknowledged that some recommendations imply adjustments of positions of doctrine or canon law. Here, however, the conference generally was cautious, accompanying the call for change by recommendations for serious study of the issues. The history of the church provides ample evidence that doctrine does develop, theological positions do prosper and wane, and laws themselves are reversed. The will of the delegates is best interpreted, then as a resolve for acceleration of this process, in response to those whose need is the greatest, and where the inequities seem most apparent.

Given the variety of reactions, especially with regard to the Detroit assembly itself, one may well wonder where the preponderance of opinion lies. A sampling of opinion after the conference, taken by the present writer, sheds some light on the question. The survey received a response from fifteen bishops, eleven religious women, six priests, and sixteen lay persons, 20 percent of the sample receiving questionnaires.

The bishops, as a group, were reserved in their analysis. They saw the process as an excellent opportunity to engage in receptive listening. They were quite varied in their estimations of the value of the goals at which the delegates arrived, responses ranging from enthusiasm to disgust. They looked forward to continued dialogue, but did not seem overly disposed to take steps toward sharing their authority itself.

Religious and lay respondents, on the other hand, were almost ecstatic in their assessment of *A Call to Action,* with a few exceptions. They were much more in agreement than the bishops in their approval of the policy recommendations voted upon. Above all, they hope for a church in which coresponsibility becomes the hallmark. Their major misgiving centered upon the possible reluctance of the bishops to act on *Call to Action's* resolutions.

The priests surveyed constituted too small a group to justify any firm inferences. Their evaluation seemed to lie somewhere between that of the bishops and the other delegates. They were supportive of the aspirations of the consultation, yet comparatively cool in their approbation.

To the extent that delegates particularized their anxieties about implementation, three salient points were observable. A number questioned whether *Call to Action* results would filter down to the local levels, especially in given dioceses and parishes. Secondly, the absence of a mechanism to hold episcopal leadership accountable was noted. Lastly, there was a feeling that if no significant action is taken until the next bishops' meeting much impetus will be lost and the cutting edge of the more incisive recommendations will be dulled.

If the church is to capitalize on the energy and dedication catalyzed by *Call to Action,* therefore, it would seem that a three stage process of implementation should be initiated "yesterday, if not sooner." The process would address the immediate, while nonetheless concentrating primarily on both short range and long range goals.

The "immediate" encompasses the current year. Within this period it should be possible for individual bishops and existing agencies to react in a responsive way to some of the conference's suggestions. Such efforts should be well-publicized, for their symbolical effect as an affirmation of the consultation's intent. At the very least they should include a sincere effort on the part of every diocese to acquaint its members with the decisions of *A Call to Action,* with accountability to the NCCB/USCC.

"Short-range" objectives would be those which might be reasonably met within two to three years. Here difficult choices must be made with regard to allocation of scarce resources. As they determine priorities, the input from all phases of the consultation process ought to be weighed carefully by the bishops. This input as it now stands would suggest an agenda for action somewhat along the following lines, with each entry to be worked out through representative participation and coresponsibility: (1) A nationwide intensive program to enrich marriage and family life, instituted and monitored wherever possible through diocesan pastoral councils; (2) accentuation of the Campaign for Human Development, with a diversified effort to increase its financial base, and with wider publicity of programs funded, with the aim of making it indisputably clear that the church itself does share its resources with the poor; (3) occasional opening of the office of preaching to the nonordained, and qualified women in particular; circulation of a methodology to be considered for use by all parishes to engage interested and competent members of each community in revitalization of homilies and other educational efforts for adults; (4) institution of affirmative action plans in all dioceses and church agencies, accompanied by research to discern the true meaning and scope of "equal opportunity" within the Catholic church; (5) an ambitious campaign to improve the quality of rural life through the National Catholic Rural Life Conference; (6) a parallel institutional effort of at least equal proportions on behalf of life in the inner city; open and decisive action on the part of church leadership to influence carefully specified governmental policies, for example, the building of a world food reserve; (7) the evaluation of each diocese of a firm in which it has a significant portion of its investments, to determine compliance with affirmative action and equal opportunity principles as well as laws, with divestment as a possible response to non-compliance; (8) strengthening of the Office of International Justice and

Peace by increased funding, and by establishment of diocesan affiliate offices; (9) sponsorship of regional forums to bring together episcopal leadership, Catholic educators, and decision-makers in interaction with leaders of the business community, and of multinational corporations in particular, to explore the implications of the free enterprise economic system for social justice, the humanizing of work, and world development; (10) demonstrations within every diocese dramatizing the church's rejection of the arms race as a path to peace; (11) design and church-wide use of liturgical celebrations emanating from the concerns surfaced through *Call to Action*, for the purpose of reconciliation and consciousness raising geared to further action, with issues deriving from injustices in ethnic, racial, and cultural domains receiving priority attention.

It is not assumed that the preceding list of conceivable activities is especially compelling. It is intended to be no more than illustrative. One might claim for it the merits of reflecting very strongly the consensus of the conference on the types of action which need to be undertaken, of being consistent with the priorities identified in the hearings and with the data submitted by parishes throughout the nation, and perhaps, most importantly, of being *doable*—given authentic willingness to act rather than simply discuss. In any event, it is only commitments and programs along these lines that will maintain the credibility of the bicentennial effort. Whatever the specific steps ultimately decided upon, relevance to the powerless and those in most dire need should be the final arbiter.

"Long-range" planning refers to activities reaching

three or more years into the future. On this level it is thorough-going reorganization of the structures of the church that must be considered if many of the commitments voted by *A Call to Action* are to be kept. So complex and massive would this task be that the church's leadership might do well to commission a secular team of experts in the science of organizational diagnosis comprehensively to study the church's many institutions and agencies. The ultimate goal would be abandonment of obsolete structures, realignment of others, and creation of new agencies where indicated, better to utilize all available resources in service of the needs so passionately identified throughout the past two years.

Just as other contemporary institutions are turning to participative management and "flatter" organizational systems, the church cannot resonate with and tap to the utmost the potential of Catholics of today's world unless it forsakes its pyramidal structures of the past, its extremely "vertical" hierarchy, in favor of more horizontal patterns of decision-making and sharing of responsibility. In other words, the imperial style and fabric of leadership appropriated from Constantine must give way to the humility of Christ, who did not consider even the prerogatives of divinity something to be clung to. Paradoxically, it seems likely that this is the *sole* manner in which the power of apostolic leadership can be preserved, as the dawn of the twenty-first century and the new demands of a new kind of people approach.

As we began this study, the twin polarities of dominance-submission and love-hate occupied our attention. In listening to the witness borne through *A Call to Action,* we have observed the many ways in which the church could move humankind towards transcendence of the dominance-submission dichotomy, above all as the people of God seeking less to be served, and offering rather to serve. We have been struck with the capacity of the church to love, as well as with its failures to do so. We have been saddened by the propensity of elements within the church to hate even other members of the Body of Christ if their values, life styles, or beliefs do not conform to standards perpetuating "establishment" priorities.

By the willingness of the bishops to engage in so original a venture for the Catholic church in the United States, and by the willingness of *A Call to Action* delegates to pour forth their hearts and souls, we have been led to hope for a new church, in which a new depth of love reconciles the hatreds and bitterness of the past. We have been presented with a vision not of what the church is, but of what it may well become.

In the last analysis, two forces will be critical: material resources and care. The church could have an infinite flow of resources, but without care there would never be sufficient wealth. With intensity of Christian love, unconditional caring, the limits to what can be achieved are unknown.

Historical evidence would suggest that Christianity's most vital years, its first three centuries, were marked neither by power, nor bureaucracy, not very sound financing. Today the same thing is true. The currency of the church is, as it was in the beginning, the quality of its faith, its love, its hope. Its one formula for success remains the same, the New Law, the beatitudes and the justice they propose as the identifying characteristic of the reign of Christ.